Guided Meditations, Bedtime Stories & Hypnosis For Deep Sleep, Self-Healing & Anxiety (2 In 1): Beginners Scripts For Insomnia, Stress-Relief, Depression, Overthinking & Happiness

By Meditation Made Effortless

Guided Meditations For Deep Sleep, Overcoming Anxiety & Mindfulness: Beginners Scripts For Self-Healing, Depression, Insomnia, Relaxation, Overthinking, Positive Thinking & Happiness

By Meditation Made Effortless

Table Of Contents

Guided Meditation for Overcoming Anxiety 1

Guided Meditation for Overcoming Anxiety 2 5

Guided Meditation for Sleep 10

Guided Meditation for Deep Sleep 2 13

Guided Meditation for Self-healing 15

Guided Meditation for Self-healing 2 18

Guided Meditation for Relaxation 22

Guided Meditation for Relaxation 2 26

Guided Meditation for Overcoming Insomnia 30

Guided Meditation for Overcoming Depression 33

Guided Meditation for Overcoming Depression 2 37

Guided Mindfulness Meditation for Overcoming Anxiety 40

Guided Meditation For Overcoming Depression 47

Guided Meditation For Stress Relief 54

Guided Meditation For Overcoming Insomnia 61

Guided Meditation For Self-healing 67

Guided Meditation for Overcoming Anxiety

Welcome to the guided meditation for overcoming anxiety. It will help you free yourself from worries and stress. I suggest you practicing it at the time of the day when you know you won't be disturbed for about 30 minutes. Find some quiet and comfortable place. I suggest you meditate lying on your back, with your hands relaxed next to the body, with your legs straight, relaxed, and slightly opened to the ceiling.

Once you are comfortable, I invite you to focus on my voice and follow my guidance. This meditation will help you release anxiety, feel relief, and find the place of peace within yourself.

Allow your body and mind to relax. Allow yourself to experience a sense of peace and release all the anxiety and disturbing thoughts. Allow thoughts to pass. You don't need them right now. There's nothing to be worried about. You are safe now.

Take a nice, deep breath, and as you're exhaling, bring your attention to this moment, to here and now. Anxiety is most often the result of focusing too much on the future, and things that didn't even happen yet, and probably never will. In this meditation, you'll learn how to bring yourself back to this moment. This moment is the only one that exists for you. At this moment, all is well.

You're in the right place, doing the right thing. You shouldn't be anywhere else and nothing else you should be doing right now.

Everything will be fine. The tension you feel will pass. You'll relax, you'll be okay, and this all will pass.

You deserve to be okay and to shake off all the anxiety. Just be present at this moment, and focus your undivided attention. Don't fight your thoughts.

Bring awareness to your body. Scan your body by focusing on each part and notice how you feel exactly.

Anxiety is certainly unpleasant, but it's not dangerous. You are safe.

Now, we'll relax the whole body, part by part. Scan your body, focusing on each part, and relaxing it. Notice where you hold the anxiety in the body, and try to relax those tensed muscles. Breathe deeply and try to relax a bit more with every exhale.

Relax your toes and feet. Relax your ankles and legs, upside to your knees. Let your heavy, tight muscles relax. Relax your hips and glutes. Now the lower half of your body is relaxed. Scan it once again and notice the parts where you might still be holding anxiety. Just remember which are those parts, we'll come back to them later.

Bring your awareness to your stomach. Notice how relaxed it is as it goes up and down with every breath. Then relax your chest. Feel your ribcage is floating.

Feel your back on the surface. Imagine your spine in perfect alignment. Then relax your back from the lowest point upside, part by part, with every exhale. Once again, take a deep breath and exhale, for the whole back relaxed. If there are any points where you are still holding some anxiety, remember it.

Then relax your hands. Start from your fingers and palms, opened to the ceiling. Relax your hands, elbows, and upper arms.

It's time to relax your shoulders. Shoulders are the most important point in relaxation - that is the place where we hold most of our worries, stress, and anxiety, and often the weight we are not even aware of. Let your shoulders relax and drop down. Let go of all the weight you were carrying on your shoulders. Permit all those concerns and stress to leave you.

Relax your neck - feel the back of your neck softens. Your throat relaxes and opens.

If there's any spot that is still tensed, make a mental note for later.

It's time to relax your head and face. Relax your ears and cheeks. Let your jaw release and relax your lips. Relax the very base of your tongue. Let your cheeks and nose relax, and all those tiny facial muscles. Your eyes are gently closed and relaxed. It feels so good to rest your eyes. Relax your eyebrows and forehead. Now, relax the top of your head. Take one more deep breath for the whole body relaxed. Scan the whole body once again, and notice all those parts that are not completely relaxed yet, where you're still might be holding anxiety. It might be your jaw, your shoulders, or the scalp. Maybe your cheeks or forehead. Check all the parts to see if there's any tension remain.

Now, imagine feeling warmth in those parts. Imagine you are made of chocolate, and now those points slowly warm up. When they are warm enough, the chocolate begins to melt. Muscles become soft and elastic, completely relaxed, and anxiety-free.

Enjoy this feeling and rest. This relaxation is your gift to yourself. That's the best thing you could be doing right now.

Scan the whole body once again—notice which part is the most relaxed one. Feel the relaxation and warmth in that part. Then imagine it spreading from that point through the whole body. Relaxed zone grows, slowly filling the whole body, and pushing out all the anxiety.

Your breathing will help you overcome anxiety. That is your most powerful tool. It will help you calm and relax. Focusing on your breathing is enough. If some thought comes, it's okay. Don't fight it, don't judge it, just put it aside. You don't need it right now.

Bring your attention to your breathing. Feel the air in your nostrils, breathing in, filling the lungs, and going out as you exhale. Just focus on your breath. Place your hands on your stomach and feel how it expands as the air pours in. Imagine the emptiness and feel the way of the air leaving your body as you're exhaling.

Stay with the breath. If you start to feel anxiety, just take another deep breath and focus on feeling it filling your lungs.

Breathe in, counting to four. One, two, three, four.

Then hold your breath, counting to three.

One, two, three.

Exhale, counting to eight.

One, two, three, four, five, six, seven, eight.

Once again:

Inhale, counting to four.

One, two, three, four.

Hold your breath, counting to three.

One, two, three.

Exhale, counting to eight.

One, two, three, four, five, six, seven, eight.

If some thought distracts you, just notice it and let it go. Bring your attention back to breathing.

Imagine the air you inhale is peace and calmness, and the air you exhale is your anxiety. Every time you exhale, you let go of tension and anxiety. You're changing it for peace and relaxation. Feel the relaxed space becomes bigger and bigger, and the space filled with anxiety shrinks and becomes smaller until it completely disappears. Notice how breathing soothes and calms you.

Now, while inhaling, mentally say to yourself: "Relax." While you're exhaling, repeat "Relax."

Once again: inhale - relax, exhale - relax.

Your body is relaxed, and your mind is calm. Thoughts are slowing down. You are safe now. Stay calm and feel in control.

Now, in a safe environment, think about how you feel when you are overflowed with anxiety. Tell yourself it's normal to feel that way when you are concerned. The next time you feel that way, remind yourself it's okay, and it will pass.

Now, let your mind relax, too. You don't have to focus on anything anymore. Just rest, relax, and trust everything will be fine.

You are at a special place now. That is the place of inner peace and serenity. There are no worries. Everything is well. Not only that you feel relief, but also, you have learned how to get there. Your breath and focus have brought you here. This is the place within you, and you can get there whenever you want. Here, you can always find shelter and rest from worries and anxiety, even in the middle of the day.

You can stay with this feeling even when you finish with meditation. This peace can stay with you throughout your usual daily activities.

The next time you start to feel anxiety, you might just remember this meditation, and it might be enough to ground you in peace. You'll be able to release anxiety and take back control, breathing deeply, relaxing, and bringing yourself to the present moment. Practicing this meditation, you'll become more and more confident. You'll know that you are bigger than anything that causes your anxiety.

You are strong. You are calm. You are free. You are peaceful. You are powerful. You are hopeful. You are positive. You are serene.

For those of you who want to go on with daily activities when the meditation is over, it's time to wake up. Slowly move your hands and toes and gently stretch. When you feel ready, open your eyes. This peace will stay with you throughout your day.

For those of you who want to fall asleep after the meditation: just go on, enjoy the music, and relaxed feeling that will lull you to sleep. When you wake up, you'll be refreshed and renewed, calm, and relaxed. Sleep well, and have nice dreams.

Guided Meditation for Overcoming Anxiety 2

Welcome to the guided meditation for relieving anxiety and changing it for peace and inner balance. In this meditation, you'll learn how to detach from your disturbing emotions and find serenity.

Before we begin, find the most comfortable position. You might want to lie on your back or side or to sit. You can sit or lie wherever it's comfy for you, but also be free to move during the meditation if you feel better that way. You are the one who knows the best what's best for you.

This is the personal time only for you. You deserve it.

Suffering from anxiety often means that you are spending too much time in your head, focusing on thoughts, and being mentally absent. Your mind is hyperactive, crazy busy, focused on the future. Meanwhile, you pay too little attention to sensations in your body and neglect your breathing. Perhaps your breath is short and shallow as if you were in a real, constant danger.

Practicing this meditation, you'll learn how to relax your body, slow your mind, and deepen your breathing. That way, your brain will understand you are safe and switch off the panic button, stopping your anxiety.

At the same time, we'll repeat some mantras to change your beliefs and remove some subconscious blockages.

Now I invite you to close your eyes and follow my voice. Bring your attention to this very moment.

Become aware of your head and try to contract tiny muscles of your scalp and the forehead. Then relax them. Relax your ears. Feel all the tension in your eyes. Then calm them, rest, and completely relax. Relax all the muscles of your face. Compress your lips, and then let them relax. Clench your jaw, and then let it loose. Tense the muscles of the back of your neck by pressing the chin against the chest. Then bring the head back and relax the neck.

Contract your shoulder muscles, and then relax them, letting the shoulders drop down in the relaxed position.

Contract the muscles of your back and then relax them, feeling how they loosen, one by one, until the whole back is relaxed. Fill your chest with air, and while you exhale, feel them relaxing.

Pull your navel to spine, and feel the abdominals tensed. Then let your stomach relax.

Clench your fists, contracting the hands, and arms. Then release the clench, relaxing your fingers, palms, wrists, and arms.

Contract your glutes, and then slowly relax them. Notice how relaxed the whole body feels.

Contract the whole legs, from hips to thighs, down to the feet and toes. Then relax your hips, relax the thighs, relax your knees. Relax cruses, relax your ankles, let your feet relax.

Now the whole body is relaxed.

Bring awareness to your breathing. You don't have to change anything, just notice breathing in and breathing out.

Imagine yourself lying on the grass. It's a beautiful sunny day. There's a clear sky above you. Take a nice, deep breath, and as you're exhaling, imagine you are making soap bubbles. The anxiety from all parts of your body leaves you, fulling the bubbles. Then picture a bubble flies into the sky, and pop out.

Inhale again, take all the anxiety you can find, and imagine blowing it into a bubble. Then send it to the sky. The bubble flies, up, up, and pops out.

Do it once again. Take a breath; let your stomach expand. Then breathe out all of the anxiety, making a lot of bubbles. They fly around you, in all directions, taking your anxiety away. You can see them popping out and disappear.

With the next breath, collect all the anxiety you might still be holding, and exhale, making a lot of bubbles. Watch them flying away.

Now listen to the affirmations I say and slowly repeat them, mentally or out loud, whichever you prefer. Dedicate one breath to each of them.

Inhale, and repeat the mantra as you're exhaling.

I'm aware of my breathing. I'm aware of the air going in and out of my body.

Inhale. Exhale.

I'm aware of my body. I'm aware of my heart rhythm.

Between each two, make space for focusing on your inhale and exhale.

I'm aware of my fears and anxiety. I'm aware of the discomfort I feel.

I'm aware of the negative thoughts that make me feel anxious.

Now, as I inhale and exhale, I'm slowly calming my mind.

I'm letting go of negative thoughts.

As I am breathing, I'm calming my anxiety.

I'm relaxing my body and slowing down my thoughts.

With each exhale, I'm letting go of fears and concerns.

With every inhale, I'm finding more peace.

I inhale calmness. I exhale peace.

Smile while you're breathing.

Being aware of my breathing, I'm letting go of everything that doesn't serve me.

I inhale serenity. I exhale joy.

I am safe and secure. I give myself permission to be in peace.

I'm well.

Things are getting better and better every day.

I expect great things to happen.

Now tell your anxiety: I see you. It's okay. I accept you and love you.

I accept all of my emotions. I allow myself to experience them. They don't define me. I can observe them while remaining calm.

When you accept your emotions, instead of fighting against them, they become lighter. When you set them free, they are able to flow through your body and leave you.

Say, "Thank you for being here to protect me. But I don't need your help anymore. I am ready to let you go now."

Notice how lighter and free you feel.

I'm healing all the time. My body and mind are in a healthy harmony.

I allow myself to be in peace.

Now imagine warm, golden light bathing and healing you, part by part, from head to toes, wrapping you in a soft glow. It's mighty, yet gentle.

I enjoy being wrapped in a soft, warm blanket. I am safe and secure. It's so good to feel the warm, soft hug.

I feel reborn and re-energized now.

I feel wellness in the whole body, in each cell of my body.

I rest in this comfort and peace. I allow myself to slip into tranquility and gentleness.

I enjoy being in this completely relaxed state, free from worries and anxiety.

Now, imagine stairs that lead down. You can picture them whatever you like. We are going downstairs.

Take a deep breath. Inhale, counting to three. One, two, three.

While exhaling, imagine you are going downstairs, counting your steps to five. One, two, three, four, five.

Inhale, counting to four. One, two, three, four.

Exhale, and move on down the stairs, counting to six. One, two, three, four, five, six.

Inhale, counting to five. One, two, three, four, five.

Exhale, counting to seven. One, two, three, four, five, six, seven.

You are in a dark room now. It's not completely dark here, but you barely can see where you're going. Don't be afraid. You are safe.

Take a few steps. You are in the center of the room. Imagine sitting on the floor, with your legs crossed. Although it's dark here, you can see there is an item on the floor, in front of you. It's a bowl.

You can pick it up. Hold it in your hands. It's heavy. Its surface is smooth and cold. You can't clearly see its color, but you know it's dark.

Now put it back on its place on the floor in front of you.

Picture your anxiety as dark sand, collected in your body.

Imagine taking your anxiety, as much of it as you can grab with your hands. Put it in the bowl. Repeat it a few times.

Imagine your worries and concerns as dark, cold stones in your mind. Take them and put them into the bowl, too.

Repeat this with each of the worries that bother you, causing your anxiety.

Now, you've put all your anxiety, worries, and negative thoughts in the bowl.

Breathe deeply, with your belly.

Everything is constantly changing.

Dark can turn into light.

Your worries and anxiety can change into acceptance, peace, love, power, and joy.

Notice the bowl becomes lighter. You can clearly see it now. It becomes lighter with each of your breaths. Dark sand becomes lighter, too; then, it starts to glow in the dark. It's a shiny powder, like a glitter. Dark stones you have put into the bowl become lighter and lighter. Now they shine brightly, like jewels. The bowl shines with bright, golden light, spreading it all over the room. You are sitting in the bright, clean light, inhaling it.

Your thoughts changed from dark and heavy to glimmering jewels, luck, wonderful possibilities. As you inhale, the whole body fulls with bright, healing light. Now you glow. You are in peace. You are love. You are light.

When a dark thought comes to you again, you can direct it into this bowl. It will turn into light. This bowl will always be here for you.

You can come back here whenever you wish.

When you are ready, you can slowly stand up and go back to the stairs. You can take the light and your bright jewels of positive thoughts with yourself.

We are going upstairs. Take a deep breath and count backward with me.

Six, five, four, three, two, one.

You are back in your usual surrounding. But with one significant change - you are calm and peaceful, you spread the light, and you know you can come back to take more of it whenever you need.

When you feel ready, take a deep breath. Exhale and gently open your eyes.

Guided Meditation for Sleep

Good evening. Welcome to the meditation that will help you fall asleep and have a good night's rest. I invite you to focus on my voice. It will guide you into a state of deep relaxation and lull you to sleep.

You might fall asleep while I'm still talking. If it happens, don't worry. Although you are sleeping, your subconscious mind is listening to what I say—listening to this meditation even while sleeping will help you relax on a deeper level and improve the quality of your rest.

The day is now ended. Experiences are over, and they drift into the past. With ease and love, turn your attention to this moment. Be present here and now. There's nothing else you should be doing right now. There's no place where you should be instead of this comfortable, warm bed. The night is here for us to have a good rest and recharge. Your body needs to reenergize, and your mind needs a break, too. It's been busy and productive all day long. Now it is time for it to rest. This guided relaxation will take you into a state when your body rejuvenates, and your mind refreshes. All you need to do is to listen to me and relax. You can relax at a fast or a slow pace, whatever is more convenient for you. You can relax your body part by part, or try to relax the whole body at once, more and more, with each breath.

So, bring your attention to here and now. Feel the warmth and peace. Feel the pillow cradling your head, and the warm, soft blanket wrapping you. Feel the comfortable surface of your mattress, the touch of your beddings.

Bring your awareness to your breath now. Take a deep breath. Feel the air going through your nostrils to your lungs, and the stomach expands. Then notice the way of the air out of your body. Let every breath be a bit deeper. With every exhale, you sink into the bed.

Smile at this moment. This is your time for relaxation and recharge. Breathe in, breathe out, and dive deeper into the relaxed feeling. Feel the soft touch of your bedding. It's more and more comfortable with each breath. Notice how pleasant it is to lie there. Breathe in, breathe out, and greet that feeling of relaxation.

You can imagine that you are in a warm, cozy nest. Or, if you like it, imagine you are lying in a floating boat on calm water. You are cradled tenderly, listening to the sounds of water, with your eyes closed.

Feel the ease, and the joy. Breathe in, breathe out, and smile to this moment and to yourself. This moment is beautiful.

Take a nice deep breath. We'll relax the whole body now. Move your attention through your body, relaxing it, part by part. Your inner smile and light move together with your focus. Begin with your toes and feet. Relax them completely, then move up to inner legs and thighs. Feel the legs gently open up to the ceiling. Relax your hips, your glutes, and the genitals. Relax your hands, beginning from very fingertips, through the knuckles, into the opened palms, through the wrists, into the hands. Relax your arms.

Turn the attention to your stomach, that easily goes up and down with every breath in and breath out. Take another deep breath, and as you're exhaling, feel your chest empties and relax all the chest muscles.

Now, feel the surface of your back. Imagine your vertebras in perfect alignment. Relax them all, one by one, starting from the lower back. It feels like a gentle massage. Each muscle relaxes, becoming soft and elastic. Take a deep breath, and while exhaling, imagine you are breathing out through your spine.

Relax your shoulders. Let go of all the worries that you've been holding through the day. If there is any tension, let it go. Is there any fear? Let it go. If there is any anger or resentment, let it go and free up your shoulders. Let them drop down and relax from all the weight.

Relax your throat and let it open, relaxing on the inside. Feel the back of your neck, and let it relax, leaving your head resting on the soft pillow. Your neck is tired from holding your head up during the day. It deserves to rest.

Relax your head. Relax the skull. Your ears work even while you sleep. But give them the relaxation they need. Let your jaw release. You don't have to look pretty; now it's time only for you and for relaxation. So, relax your mouth, your lips, and tongue. Relax your cheeks, and let them rest from any tension. Relax the forehead and the top of your head. Your eyes need a good rest, too. They are already closed but now becalm them completely, and let them sink in the head. It feels so good to calm the tired eyes.

Now, visualize the surface of your whole body and relax your skin. It also needs recharge and rejuvenation.

Imagine your body on the inside. Imagine your organs working for you all the time. Mentally send them love and let them relax.

Now, give your emotions permission to let go. Let go of any sadness, any anger, jealousy. Any fear, worry, concern - let them go. Don't be hard on yourself, or the others - if there's anything to be forgiven, forgive it and let it go. Don't hold the grudge. Don't overthink, beating yourself up for your mistakes. Accept them as a part of the learning process. Forgive yourself and let it go.

There are probably thoughts running through your head. Try just to let them pass by you. It's perfectly normal to have some thoughts or see pictures while you're trying to relax. Just notice them and let them go or set them aside for another time. You don't need them right now. There's nothing you should be doing right now. You don't need to be productive, nor to accomplish anything right now. The night is here for rest. The best you can do for yourself and for the next day is to have a good recharge.

Imagine your mind as a spinning wheel. It spins around at the pace of your thoughts. Visualize how it slows down. It spins slower and slower until it stops. Your mind is calm. Your mind is clear. It's in a state of relaxation now. It's ready to step into the dreaming state.

Inhale, and with exhale, let go of everything you don't need, you don't love, and everything that bothers you. Shake it off and clear with the inner light spreading through your body.

Don't engage in any thought that comes to you. Stay calm, focused on your relaxation, and just observe. Observe your body while it's relaxing.

Watch your breathing without the urge to change anything. There's nothing you should do but relaxing and rest. It's so nice to be like this, feeling tucked in a cozy, warm nest, or floating in a boat, doing nothing but being present.

Inhale deeply. Then exhale, feeling again your body is relaxing on a deeper level. All you don't need fades away. You are carefree. All is well, peaceful, and easy.

Breathe in, breathe out.

You have all the time in the world. You don't needto rush anywhere. Everything is in the right place, and everything happens when the time is perfect. You have time for everything. All is well.

Give all your worries and concerns into divine hands. Leave everything to higher intelligence, and trust all will be well.

Smile with your inner smile to yourself and life.

Feel the serenity and carefreeness.

There's nothing but harmony at this moment.

Breathe in, breathe out. Feel comfort. Your body and your mind are enjoying like you're being in a mental spa.

Sink into a deeper sleep, knowing everything is fine. Let yourself step into a dreaming state.

Sleep well, and have sweet dreams.

Guided Meditation for Deep Sleep 2

Good evening. It's nice to be with you and preparing for sleep. I suggest you lye in bed and find a comfortable position. Make yourself as warm and comfortable as possible. Listen to my voice and follow the instructions, but don't stress yourself over falling asleep. Sometimes, we fall asleep fast and easily. Other times, we need to wait a little bit for sleep to come. It's okay, even if you stay awake during the whole meditation. You will relax and rest, and it will benefit your body and mind, the same way sleep does.

Bring your attention to this moment. It's time for rest, to be calm and prepare for sleep. Appreciate this moment you have only for yourself. Enjoy your comfortable bed, your mattress, your pillow, and beddings. Feel the peace and warmth. Be thankful for the day that passed. Feel appreciation for all the good that happened during the day. Now, let it go and give it to the past. Turn to the present moment with undivided attention.

Be aware of your breathing. Breathe in, feel the air going through your body, and leaving it as you exhale. Feel the tensed parts of your body. It's time to relax. Inhale, and try to feel your scalp. Then exhale slowly, relaxing the top of your head. Breathe in, and breathing out, relax your ears and jaw. With the next breath, turn your attention to your mouth. Breathe out slowly, relaxing your chin, your lips, and your tongue. Inhale. Exhale, relaxing your cheeks and nose. Feel the tension in your forehead and eyebrows. Breathe in, and breathing out, let them relax. With the next breath, relax your eye muscles. Let your eyes calm down and rest. Inhale. Exhale, and relax the whole head once again.

With the next breath, become aware of your neck and throat. Exhaling, relax them. Relax the front side, relax your throat, and let it soften and open. Relax the back of your neck. It doesn't need to do its job now. Your neck needs rest.

Take a deep breath, and breathing out, relax your shoulders. Let them drop all the weight they've been carrying through the day.

Breathe in and fill your lungs with air. Breathe out and let your chest drop down and relax completely.

Inhale and full the stomach with air. Exhale, and let your belly relax completely.

Now, breathe in, and feel the muscles of your back. Exhale, and relax the lower back. Inhale. Exhale, and relax the upper back. Breathe in, and devote breathing out to relaxation of the whole back. Visualize how all the tension from your back is going out through your spine.

With the next inhale, acknowledge the tension in your hips, glutes, and genitals. With the exhale, release it. Let your hips relax. Let your glutes relax. Let your genitals relax.

Breathe in, and feel the tension in your legs.

Exhale, and let the thighs relax.

Inhale. Exhale, and relax your legs. Let them open up a bit towards the ceiling. Let your ankles and feet relax. Relax your toes. Take a deep breath, and with the exhale, feel the whole legs relaxed.

Take a deep breath, and if there's any tension, remain in the body, let it go with the exhale.

Now, visualize you are on a mountain, in a beautiful, green forest. It's late afternoon. You are tired of a long day of walking in nature. You need to get to the little rented cottage at the bottom of the mountain. There is a comfortable, warm bed, waiting for you. But first, you need to get there. So, you're going forward, down through the forest. Imagine the green color of trees, and a small, narrow path you're stepping on. You can hear birds singing. You can see golden sunlight going through tree crowns. You are tired.

Your legs are sleepy. They need rest.

You're slowly going down, down the hill. You are daydreaming about a cozy pillow and a warm blanket. You feel the sleepiness in your hands too. And you begin to yawn.

The day will soon be over. The evening is about to come. Birds are singing, and preparing to settle in their nests. You'd like to lye down and sleep now. But you have to move forward, down, and down, to get to the cottage before the sun goes down and the dark covers the forest. The path leads down. The forest is peaceful. You can hear the sounds of nature - soft wind in the leaves and grass, the sound of your steps, birds' singing in the crowns, Baum-crickets chirr in the grass.

You're going down the path, wishing only to get to the cottage soon and sink into a comfortable bed. Your legs are tired. Your back wants to lye down and rest.

Take a deep breath, and start counting your steps down the path through the forest. Inhale, counting to four. Exhale, and count your steps down the path: one, two, three, four, five, six.

You're yawing, wishing to come to the bed soon. Breathe in again, count to four: one, two, three, four. Breathe out, and count your steps down the path: one, two, three, four, five, six. The evening's here. It becomes darker and darker in the forest. Sounds are becoming softer. The whole forest is becoming quiet. Nature goes to sleep. You can see the moon and stars in the dark sky. Moonlight is the only light now. You are close to the cottage. Just a few steps more down the path, and you're there. Your body is about to fall asleep. Your mind is calm and clear. Your legs are heavy, and you can barely walk.

Take a nice, deep breath. Let's count as you are breathing out. One, two, three, four, five, six. You are so sleepy now that you can barely count. Inhale. Exhale. One, two, three, four, five, six. You are finally here. You are opening the door of the cottage. Here is your bed, waiting for you. You can lay down now, on the cozy bedding. Place your head on a soft pillow and wrap yourself in a warm blanket. It's time to sleep now.

Your head is sleeping. Your eyes are sleeping. Your lips are relaxed and sleep finally. Your back muscles are heavy. They relax now and fall asleep. You can feel heavy leg muscles falling asleep. Your hands are lying relaxed by your body. They are falling asleep, par by part. Your whole body is sleeping now. Your mind is sleeping. Your emotions are free.

Guided Meditation for Self-healing

Welcome to the meditation for self-healing. Whether you don't feel well, or you have a diagnose, suffer from chronic pain, this meditation will help you use the ability of your body to heal itself. During this meditation, you'll be talked down into a relaxed state. From that place, you can talk to your body, send love to it, and empower it to heal.

For best results, practice this meditation as often as you can. You can heal yourself during a day, or while you are sleeping. Even if you fall asleep during the meditation, your subconscious mind will listen to my words and help your body in self-healing.

Now, make yourself comfortable. You should be pleasantly warm. Place one hand onto your heart and feel its beat. Let your body slow and get into a relaxed state. Gently relax your body. Feel how it begins to soften.

Imagine warm, golden light spreading through your body. It enters your muscle tissues and sinks into your bones. Your body loosens and relaxes. The golden light goes through your feet and lower legs, knees, moving slowly up, to your thighs and hips, stomach. It goes further up, to encompass and soothe your whole body. Feel the warmth of the golden light in your hands and arms, in your back, shoulders, neck, and in your head. Enjoy this sense of relaxation. That's the best thing you can do for yourself and your body. That state leads to healing. Knowing it, go on with relaxation until the whole body is completely relaxed, and you feel as if you were floating. The whole body is now full of bright, golden light. It wraps all of your organs and systems, radiating in all directions, and shining through your skin. Visualize your relaxed body shinning with the golden light.

You know that this light takes away all the negativity, all the toxins from your body, and all toxic emotions. It takes off all the weight that you were carrying on your shoulders, all the negative thoughts, all the worries, doubts, all the concerns. It takes away all the anger and resentment, jealousy, and hatred, that might be hiding, lingering in corners of your mind.

Imagine you are walking in nature, on a warm summer evening. The temperature of the air is perfect. You can hear insects and birds. Trees and flowers grow along the path, and their leaves are singing—everything's calm. The path flows away, carrying you.

Now, you can see a huge tree in front of you. It's old, but strong and healthy. Its crown is large, and it offers a home for many birds, squirrels, and insects, and wonderful shade during warm, sunny days. It's so tall that it seems to reach the sky, and its root goes deep into the land, to connect with the source of life. Imagine you are hugging the stem. You are attaching to its mighty life power. You are connecting with the higher intelligence through the crown that touches the sky. And you are grounding yourself through its root, deep in the ground. Feel the green, life power flowing through your body, from the top of the head to the toes, and in the opposite direction.

You sit down under the tree. Listen to the sounds of nature. Green wood supports you. Take a deep breath and bring your awareness to your body. Think about all those wonderful things that your body does every moment each day to bear you through your life. Give it an appreciation for what it does for you. It works even when you rest. There is a higher intelligence within your body. It beats your heart and pumps your blood through the veins. It digests your food and nourishes your cells. It protects you from the inner world and holds your beautiful soul. Appreciate all of that, and consciously tell your body: I love you—everything in the world responses to the vibration of love. Plants and animals, even water, responds to love. Your body is not an exception; it's majorly built by the water. Imagine how it reacts to your words. Send it lots of love and affection.

Thank your legs for bringing you through this beautiful world. Thank your hands for serving you for so many years. Thank your stomach for digesting food for you. Thank your back for supporting you, keeping you straight. Thank your neck for holding and moving your head. It's such a precious blessing to be able to move, to walk, to be able to turn left and right. Thank your brain for being such a wonderful personal assistant and such a powerful central. Thank your mouth for being able to talk, to express yourself, to feel tastes, and to kiss. Thank your nose for helping you breathe and your eyes for being able to see all the amazing things around you. Let the gratefulness fill your heart.

Repeat these words, mentally or out loud: Body, I love you. I accept and appreciate you. I know you do the best you can. I want you to be well and healthy. You deserve the best, and you deserve to function perfectly. I pour my love in you. You deserve it, and you are amazing. I pour love in every organ, every muscle, and every bone. I pour love into every system and each cell of you because I love you. I pour love into you. I give you blessings. I pour energy and health into you.

I trust you; you know how to heal yourself. I invite your wisdom and let you do what is best for you.

Take a few deep, purposeful breaths. Then allow your breath to settle in its usual pace. Allow the power of infinite love and thankfulness to unleash your body's extraordinary abilities for healing. You can heal completely.

Allow yourself to feel infinite love. Allow that sensation of love, purity, softens, and the warmth rise in your heart. Feel unconditional and eternal love. Feel connected and completed. Stay with that sensation. Then allow that feeling spread from your heart, powerful as sunlight, through the whole body. Let your body soak it up.

Now, you can name a particular part of your body that needs some extra love and attention. Pour love in that part, which needs to heal. Imagine the golden, healing light pouring into that part, overflowing it and shining from the inside. This light baths the part that needs special attention, taking off all the issues and pain. It brings balance and perfect harmony. The light is healing that part and your whole body. It restores everything in the ideal condition, as when you were born to this world. You were such a perfect baby! Your body deserves to work as it's meant to- perfectly. Absolute health is your natural condition and your inborn right. You are created to be unique, complete, and absolutely healthy. And your body knows how to restore exactly all of its functions and to cure itself.

Feel how peaceful it is now. Feel how your body is enjoying this relaxed state. It's sending you thanks now. It's grateful for this time and for the trust you are showing to it. This is what your body needs. It needs peace and calmness, time with no worries, time of serenity, and rest to reenergize and refresh. It needs it to gain energy to heal itself. It is grateful for this time you are giving to it and will show appreciation by healing and being there for you.

Whenever you feel some pain or have any health issues, visualize this healing, golden light bathing your body, and send a lot of love into the part that needs healing or pour it into the whole body. Your body knows the best way to regain perfect balance and harmony for every, even tiniest part of it.

Guided Meditation for Self-healing 2

Welcome to the guided meditation for self-healing. I recommend you do it in a lying position, using earphones. In this meditation, you can engage in your healing. All you need to do is to accept healing energy into every part of your body. When the meditation is over, you can allow this energy to continue with healing for hours, days, even weeks.

Choose time and space when you won't be disturbed for about 30 minutes.

Slowly calm yourself before this healing journey begins. Let's do a short breathing exercise. Breathe through your nose, counting to six. One, two, three, four, five, six. Then exhale through your mouth, to the count of ten. One, two, three, four, five, six, seven, eight, nine, ten. If you can't reach those numbers, don't be concerned in any way. Do what is convenient.

Repeat this for a short while. And then, let yourself flow into your natural breathing pattern. While inhaling, imagine you are breathing in a beautiful, glittering light. Breathing out, exhale all worries and negativity. Feel how your body is more and more relaxed with each exhale.

Imagine you are lying in a beautiful, green garden full of colorful flowers. You're listening to insects in grass, birds, and wind in the trees. Feel the peace and serenity.

Now, we'll relax the whole body. Breathe slowly and deeply. Concentrate on your feet. Relax your feet. Relax your toes, heels, whole feet. Relax your ankles, lower legs. Feel your legs relaxing. Relax your knees. Bring your focus to your thighs - the front and the backside of them. Feel how your thighs are more and more relaxed with each exhale. Your toes, heels, and feet - relaxed. Your ankles, lower legs, knees, and thighs - relaxed.

Put your attention to your hips, glutes, and pelvic area. Relax your glutes and observe how, with every breath, your glutes and hips are more relaxed. And, with them, the whole lower half of the body is relaxed, too.

Bring your awareness to your hands. Relax your fingers and palms. Relax your wrists. Relax your forearms, relax your elbows, and your upper arms. Your palms and fingers - relaxed, your wrists - relaxed. Your forearms, elbows, and upper arms - all are relaxed.

Bring your attention to your stomach and chest. Observe how they easily move in the rhythm of your breathing. Relax your chest completely. Relax your stomach. Focus on your lower back. Relax your lower back. Feel the surface under your back, and relax your back, part by part, from the lower back, slowly moving up, to the shoulders.

Feel the peace. Feel how your body is giving you thanks for those moments. How much good is happening right now!

Relax your shoulders. The most crucial part of relaxation is the shoulders. Relax them and let them loose. Observe how they are more and more relaxed with every exhale. Notice how, by relaxing the shoulders, you are loosening the whole body. Feel the relief.

Relax your neck. Relax the top of your head. Relax your forehead. Relax your ears. Relax your cheeks. Relax your lips and let your jaw loose. Cand relax your eyes. Relax eye muscles completely.

Breathe deeply and feel the peace. Your body is relaxed now.

Now, imagine a small, white cloud above you. It's a beautiful cloud, and it's here only for you. It brings you healing. The cloud is right above your head. Are you excited? Do you feel happy about what is coming?

It's beginning to rain from the cloud. It's a rain of light. Feel the drops on your face. It's a healing rain. You can imagine it as you want, like a light, small crystals, or pure water. Connect it with healing.

Your whole head is shining now in healing light. Enjoy it. You know what's going on now. The clod moves down, above your neck. The raindrops fall over your neck. It starts shining, too. Now, your head and the neck shine.

The cloud moves down, above your shoulders, chest, and stomach. Feel the rain. Feel the healing. Watch yourself glowing - your head, neck, shoulders, chest, and stomach. The cloud is expanding above your arms. Your arms and hands begin to shine. The cloud is growing, and now it's above your hips, pelvis, glutes, and genitals. Those parts are shining in the healing light now. Your head is shining, your neck, shoulders, chest, stomach, your arms, legs, hips, and glutes. The cloud is moving down, and raindrops are falling over your legs. Observe your legs begins to shine. Do you feel the rain? Can you feel how it serves you, and what's its purpose? The white, healing cloud is now above your whole body, and it's the same size as it. It's raining over your whole body, and all the parts are shinning. This moment, the healing raindrops on each part of your body. It's a rain of light, rain of health, and you shine brightly. Say thanks to this moment. Feel grateful for the healing that's happening right now. If you have some health challenges, you can now bring your little white cloud above the par that needs healing. If you don't have any particular health issue, let the rain falls all over your body. Visualize yourself shining.

If you have brought the healing cloud above a particular part of your body, imagine it's lighting. It's shining, and it works perfectly. All the cells of your body are happy for bringing back the balance which your body deserves.

Right now, you are giving an incredible gift to your body. The body is thankful, and it is going to show you appreciation. Enjoy this feeling and the insight that healing is going on right now.

Any tension remains in the body now releases itself in the light's comfort as it spreads through every cell and every atom. As the rain of light drops all over your body, your skin may tingle or feel warm. You feel all the stress and pain draining away under the drops of light.

The soft light is enveloping you, and spreading out, warm, and powerful.

Enjoy the relaxation and feeling that the rain brought. Rest in it, allowing it to do its work of healing you.

You are filled with pure, loving energy. See the light radiating from the center of your body.

From this relaxed state, while your body is healing itself using the infinite wisdom, you can send yourself loving thoughts to support the healing process. It's time to release the old negative thinking patterns that caused disease in your body and to adopt new ones, and build perfect, vibrant health. Listen to my voice as I am repeating positive statements. Allow these ideas to enter your subconscious and help you build positive, new patterns that create health in your body and mind.

Repeat my words mentally or just listen to these affirmations and let them become your new beliefs.

I am healing my body and mind.

I am one with life.

Perfect health is my birthright.

I forgive all those I need to forgive.

I forgive myself.

I feel growing love for myself.

I take care of myself because I love myself.

I am choosing health for my body, mind, and spirit.

I am grateful for my amazing body and all the wonderful things it does every day.

I am grateful for my healthy body and healthy mind.

I am calm and strong.

I am completely healthy.

All the cells of my body are healthy and vibrant.

I am full of positive energy.

I am full of life.

I am loved. I am enough. I am complete.

I am always healing and feel good.

I am letting go of everything that doesn't serve my highest good.

I am letting go of fear. I am letting go of anger, blame, sorrow, guilt, jealousy, blame, tension.

I am in peace. There's no need to struggle.

I am a wonderful expression of life.

I have the power within me, and it's the same power that has created me.

Now, I allow that power to heal my body and mind.

The past has no power over me. I'm letting go of it now.

I am unique and magnificent.

I am worthy of love just because I exist.

I accept and appreciate myself.

I'm willing to heal. I deserve all the best life has to give me. I deserve to be perfectly healthy.

I am in perfect balance and in harmony with the world. I allow divine energy circulates throughout my body and helps it use higher intelligence to heal.

Take a nice, deep breath and exhale, imaging flowers and grass around you.

When ready, gently come out of meditation, and continue your day. Or, if you wish, let yourself drift off to sleep.

Guided Meditation for Relaxation

Welcome to the meditation for deep relaxation.

You can practice this meditation whenever you feel tense, or just want to relax and have some calm time.

My voice will gently guide you to a relaxed state. From there, you can easily drift off to sleep or move on with your usual daily activities.

Find some quiet space where you can be alone for about half an hour. Settle down, sitting or lying, and make yourself comfortable. Close your eyes. Let the relaxation journey begin.

Take a deep breath through your nose, into your belly. Hold the breath for a moment, and then breathe out slowly through your mouth. Breathing out more slowly than breathing in can help you relax. It works as a signal to your mind that everything is well and you are safe. You can use this technique in everyday life whenever you need to calm down and relax.

Breathe in. Slowly breathe out.

Do it once again. Now, let your breathing flow in its natural pattern. Enjoy this experience. This time is only for you. Allow yourself to enjoy it. You deserve time to be committed to yourself. Allow yourself to relax.

Notice the way of your breath, through your nose into the lungs. Feel it going in, expanding your abdominals, and feel it releases, and abdominals contract.

Release any expectations. Don't expect certain things to happen during this meditation, or some insights to come. Just be present and focused on the present moment. You don't need to do anything now. You don't need to be productive, nor to think. If you still have some thoughts or internal chatters, don't be concerned in any way. It's perfectly normal to have thoughts going through your mind, or inner talk. Notice them, but don't engage. Stay aside and observe them passing by. The internal chatter and random thoughts that are popping up will slowly fade away into the background, and you won't notice them so much. Don't bother about it. Your mind is meant to produce thoughts, and it can't be just turned off immediately. It requires some time and practice to get used to relaxation and having some time when it's free from duty.

Now, imagine you're walking up a hill. It's a beautiful sunny day. The temperature of the air is pleasant. The air is fresh. You get to the top of the hill. It's a semi-magical place. From there, you can gaze at far away distance. You can see the high mountains around and the glittering river down in the valley. The sky is clear, blue, with white fluffy clouds here and there.

Visualize you are lying down, into the thick, green grass. It's soft, like a large pillow under your body. You are completely safe and serene. The air from the mountains is so pure that it's sparkling. Breathe in, imaging it filling your body. Exhale slowly.

Now, lying on the grass, bring your awareness to your body and allow it to relax completely. Start from your toes and feet. Relax them and allow them to open up a little bit to the sky. Feel the grass gently tinkling your feet. Relax your ankles. Let your calf relax. Move slowly upward, and relax your knees and thigh muscles. Feel the backside of your thighs on the ground. Your muscles become heavier with every exhale. Relax your glutes, feeling the touch of the grass and the ground below you. Let your hips loosen and relax.

Your hands are lying beside your body, straight, opened to the sky. Relax your fingers, one by one. Feel the tingling in your fingertips. Relax your palms. Let all the tension disappear from your hands. Whatever you've been holding to, let it go now. Your hands are busy all the time. They serve you and do so much for you. They deserve a relaxation. We often hold strongly to our directions in life, for some opinions and beliefs. Let everything go from your hands. Feel the soft breeze on your opened palms. Doing this, you are making space for great new energy to flow in, and you are welcoming it. Relax your wrists. Feel the touch of the grass on your forearms. Relax them. Relax your elbows, and feel them becoming flexible. Release all the tension from your upper arms. Feel the arm muscles soften.

Bring your awareness to your belly. Notice it easily expands with your inhale, like a balloon, and contracts with every exhale. Let your chest relax. Feel your ribcage floating.

It's time to relax your back. Feel the grass and the ground supporting your back. Start relaxing from the glutes, up, part by part. Feel your back muscles and let them loose, one by one. Visualize breathing in through your spine, and exhaling through it, relaxing your back.

Let your shoulders relax, loosen, and release them from your ears. We often carry the weight of all the worries and stress on our shoulders without being aware of it. Let all the weight fall from your shoulders and fly away.

Relax your neck and your throat. Relax the back of your head, while the green, soft grass is cradling it like a pillow.

Hear the breeze in the grass and trees. Hear the birds singing and insects in the grass. Now, relax your ears. Relax your scalp and your forehead. Relax your cheeks. Let your jaw release and relax your lips. Relax even the base of your tongue.

Release tension from your eyebrows and relax all the tiny muscles around your eyes. Calm your eyes and let them sink into the head. It feels so good to rest your eyes.

Bring attention to the surface of your body, and allow your skin to relax. Visualize your skin resting and reenergizing.

Now, visualize your internal organs relaxing. Every system in your body, each organ, and all the cells are resting and relaxing now, rejuvenating, and gaining fresh energy.

Your whole body is relaxed now.

Feel the grass and the surface under your body. Feel grounded and supported. Mentally say thanks to the ground for supporting and holding you. Smile. Smile to yourself, to the ground, and to this moment of relaxation. Say thank you to yourself for this beautiful present you're giving to your body, mind, and soul. This relaxation is what your body needs the most. It will show you its appreciation through serving and supporting you even better.

Feel strongly grounded, yet floating on the soft grass. It's now time to allow all the weight you've been carrying, all the hard, dark emotions and thoughts go to the ground. Imagine them like dark sand, pouring out from your body, and going to the ground. You can name your worries or hard feelings, and tell it: I'm letting you go now. I'm devolving you to the ground. Repeat this as many times as you wish, for every concern, and every negative emotion you want to get rid of.

It's time to relax your mind now. It's normal to have some thoughts, don't worry. They come and go. When it's relaxed, the mind notices them and let them pass by. You don't have to engage in any of them. It's not the time for thinking, analyzing, or following any thought. Stay outside of them and observe them from a distance. This might be new for your mind. It's used to work all the time, to follow every thought that pops up, and to trust them. Now, you are letting your mind rest and see your thoughts for what they really are - only thoughts. You can blow them away like a dandelion. They are not the truth itself, but just creations of your mind. Now, look at the blue sky above you. It's a wonderful sunny day. The sky is almost clear, but you can notice fluffy white clouds here and there. Some of them are even greyish as if they are carrying rain. You know what those clouds mean - they represent your thoughts. Those fluffy and white are your positive thoughts, and neutral ones - thoughts about what you need to do, where to go, different ideas popping up in your mind. Those greyish and rainy ones are here to represent your negative, difficult thoughts, worries, and fears.

You can feel a fresh breeze on your skin. It's certainly far stronger in the highs because you see the clouds are moving. The wind brings them away, and they disappear from your view, one by one. They carry your thoughts away. One by one, they disappear, and the sky remains clear blue, as your mind, too. Your inner mental space is clear. Your mind is calm, resting, and enjoying the silence and the scene of a clear blue sky.

Now, you've got up from the soft grass and standing the hill, gazing to the distance. The fresh breeze rising from the mountains around becomes stronger and turns into the wind. It's pleasantly cold, and it brings purity of mountain air. Take a deep breath. Fill your lungs with purity and freshness. Inhale deeply, and, if any tension and unwanted emotions are remaining, release them with exhale. Whatever you don't need anymore, let it go away into the cleansing wind. The wind takes away all the remaining tension, all the negativity you haven't sent to the ground while lying on the grass. If you have any thoughts or beliefs that don't serve you anymore - let them go with the wind. Any sadness, anger, resentment, jealousy, fear, any sour emotions - let them be taken away by the wind and disappear into nothingness.

The wind becomes stronger and stronger. It blows now not only over you but through you. It blows through your clothes, and your skin, through your muscles tissues and bones. All you don't want is carried away from you. You experience being cleansed by the cool wind. Allow yourself to experience this, to feel the purity of the wind, its power, and cleanliness, with whole your being.

Breathe in, visualizing freshness filling your lungs. Exhale, releasing all mental and physical weight. It's time to get rid of everything you don't want - the wind will carry it away. This is time only for you to reenergize and be cleaned mentally and physically to get fresh energy, thoughts, and ideas flow in.

Say, mentally or out loud: "I breathe in health."

"I breathe out, and name things you want to release."

"I breathe in wellbeing."

"I breathe out," and again name things you want to let go.

Repeat this a few times, for everything you want to go away with the cleansing wind.

Feel the wind flowing around you and through you. Feel the flow and be a part of it. Enjoy this experience for a while.

Eventually, the wind drops back to a soft breezing. Your cleansing and healing are done. You feel pure, lite, new, and energized. Your body is completely relaxed and renewed. Your mind is fresh and clear.

When you feel ready, softly open your eyes. You can return to your usual daily activities, or drift off to sleep.

Whenever you want to be completely cleansed and reenergized, or just relaxed, you can come back. This hill, mountains, the soft grass, and the cleansing wind will be here for you.

Guided Meditation for Relaxation 2

Welcome to the meditation that will help you relax your body and mind on a deeper level.

Relaxation is precious, but most of us lack it in our usual daily lives. We often go through our days with tensed shoulders and tension held in other body parts. We are even not aware of it until we relax and realize how much weight we have been carrying.

When we relax, so much good is happening. Our body needs to be regularly relaxed and free of any tension. Our mind needs a break. We don't allow new energy and prosperity to flow into our life while we are tensed. We need to open up to the flow of energy so that we could be included in it. Relaxation is tremendously beneficial for your body and mind, and all the aspects of life.

It's a part of self-care. Self-care is not selfish at all. It's the way to take care of yourself, so you could take care of the others, too. It is for your highest good, but also for the highest good of all the people around you.

This is time only for you. You deserve it. Allowing yourself to relax is the best thing you can do for yourself, and it doesn't matter how much things are waiting for you. Relaxation will improve your productivity and the quality of every action you take. So, allow yourself to enjoy these moments.

I invite you to follow my guidance.

Choose a place and the time of a day or night when you know you won't be disturbed. Sit or lie down and make yourself comfortable. You can use a blanket to make yourself warm if needed. The temperature should be pleasant.

Give yourself a few moments to calm and slow down before this journey. Take a few deep breaths. While breathing out, relax the whole body a bit more.

Imagine you are on a beautiful beach. It's a beautiful sunset. You are walking barefoot along the beach, feeling sand through your toes. It's warm, soft, and feels like massaging your feet.

The air is warm and has a fresh seaside smell. You can feel a salty breeze on your face. Breathe in and let it fill your lungs.

Now slowly breathe out.

Repeat it once again.

Breathe in.

Slowly breathe out.

Now, you decide it's enough walking, and you want to rest.

Sit or lie down on the soft sand. As the sun is beginning to set, the sand got beautiful, golden shine. It's smooth, and it shapes to support your body. Make yourself comfortable.

Listen to the waves rolling in. It's one of the most relaxing sounds in the world. Waves curl over and dissolve into foam.

Breathe deeply, with your belly, and focus on the sounds of the waves. Let go of the urge to do something. There's nothing else you should be doing right now. Just enjoy the touch of the soft surface under your back, your legs, your hands. Notice how the smooth sand is cradling your head like a pillow. Breathe with your stomach and listen to the sounds of the sea.

Bring your attention to your breath. Breathe in to the count of four. One, two, three, four.

Hold it to the count of three. One, two, three.

Breathe out, counting to seven. One, two, three, four, five, six, seven.

Repeat - breathe in to the count of four.

One, two, three, four.

Hold your breath to the count of three - one, two, three.

Exhale, to the count of seven - one, two, three, four, five, six, seven.

Do it once again.

Inhale, counting to four.

Hold, counting to three.

Exhale, to the count of seven.

Now, let your breathing settle in its natural pattern.

Bring awareness to your body. Notice how your body feels. Can you detect any tension? Notice where you hold it in the body.

Mentally thank your body for serving you, for being there for you, holding your beautiful soul.

Let's relax the whole body, part by part.

Inhale, while tensing your feet. Then exhale, and relax them. Relax your toes, your heels, your whole feet, and ankles.

Tense your crus muscles. Tight them as strong as you can, and then, with an exhale, lose them up. Squeeze your thigh muscles. Exhaling, let them relax. Relax your whole legs, from feet to cruses to knees to thighs.

Squeeze your glutes. Then, let them relax. Relax your hips and your pelvic area.

Bring awareness to your hands. Feel the sand below them. Thank your hands for serving you for so many years. Stretch your fingers, and then relax them. Relax your palms, opened to the sky. Stretch the muscles of your hands, and then relax them - your wrists, your forearms, your elbows, up to your arms.

Bring your attention to your abdominals. Notice your stomach is relaxed, as it expands and contracts in the rhythm of your breathing. Feel the peace in your abdominal area.

Fill your lungs with a deep breath. Breathing out, let them relax.

Now, stretch your back. With an exhale, let all the muscles of your back lose. Imagine two gentle hands massaging your back, from the bottom to the top. Feel the warmth in each muscle as you're focusing on it.

Relax your shoulders. Let them drop away from your ears.

Tense your neck. Then, counting backward from 10, relax your neck, your shoulders, and your throat.

Notice the tension in your head and facial muscles.

Relax the back of your head.

Raise your eyebrows, and tense your forehead and your scalp. Breathing out, relax your scalp, your forehead, and eyebrows.

Tense all the facial muscles, and then relax them - all the tiny muscles around your eyes, your cheeks, your lips. It feels so good to rest your eyes.

Your whole body is completely relaxed now.

Enjoy this feeling. Feel the rays of the setting sun on your skin, and the warmth of the sand everywhere under your body.

Now, visualize, you are opening your eyes. You are stretching your muscles and getting up. You feel energized and renewed.

You wish to bath in the sea. You know that this bath is going to be healing and relaxing. The sea surface is still and sparkling. You are stepping into the water. Imagine a golden, healing liquid entering your feet, your legs, and moving up through your body, as you are going deeper into the sea. Now, the whole body is full of golden water as you are swimming in the sea. Everything you don't want drains out from your body and disappear in a deep blue. All the old energy from your body is replaced with the new, fresh one. Feel free to dive into the water. All the thoughts and worries from your head flow out to the water. Your mind is clear and refreshed.

You are floating on the water. Feel the lightness and being gently supported by the sea. You are completely relaxed on a deep level.

When you feel ready, swim out to the beach. You are wrapping yourself in a huge, soft towel. Feel its comforting warmth.

When the meditation is finished, you'll feel completely relaxed, re-energized, and renew. You can go on with your daily activities or fall asleep.

When you are ready, gently open your eyes. Or, if you want, drift off to deep slumber, and have nice dreams.

Guided Meditation for Overcoming Insomnia

Welcome to the guided meditation for overcoming insomnia. If you have trouble with falling asleep from time to time or quite often, this meditation is for you.

Use it in the evening before sleep. Lie in your bed, and make yourself comfortable. You can lie on your back or on the side, whatever is convenient. Listen to my voice. I will guide you to a relaxed state, from where you can easily drift off to sleep.

My suggestions will impact your subconscious mind and help you fall asleep easier but also stay asleep during the night. You'll sleep with a deeper slumber without waking up during the night. You will finally get a proper night's rest.

Falling asleep and staying asleep during the whole night is a habit. And like every other habit, it requires some time and practice to be established. You can use this meditation every night until you form a habit and overcome insomnia.

After a night of deep sleep, you will wake up refreshed and renewed.

If you have hard times falling asleep because you are overthinking, some concerns bother you, or you endlessly repeat your to-do list in your mind, I'll suggest you press stop now, and write it all down. Whatever it is, put it down, download from your busy mind and put aside. You'll deal with it tomorrow. Now, it's time for relaxation, rest, and recharge.

Bring your focus to this moment, and your comfortable bed, here and now. Relaxing and listening to my voice is all you need to do now. It will lull you to sleep.

Take a deep breath, hold it to the count of three. Then, release.

Do it once again - take a breath, hold it, counting to three. One, two, three. Then exhale.

One more time - breathe in deeply, hold it to the count of three. Then, breathe out.

Don't force it in any way; just do what's pleasant. Let your breathing drop back to its natural pattern.

Allow your body to lose and become more relaxed with each exhale.

Now, watch your thoughts flowing by. Having a busy mind means being preoccupied and having thoughts raise up like bubbles all the time.

Realize those are just thoughts. You are not your thoughts. Those are just products of your busy mind. Your mind is slowing down now. There will be fewer and fewer thoughts as your mind becomes slower and slower in producing them.

Since a busy mind is used to work all the time, you can't just banish it to produce thoughts. But what you can do is to focus on something else. You can't think two thoughts at the same time, so you need to occupy your mind with certain thoughts. Focusing on mindful thoughts will push away unwanted ones.

Bringing awareness to your body and focusing on physical sensations will keep you grounded.

Bring awareness to your body. Be mindful of how it feels. Feel the support your body gets from your bed. Feel the comfort and softness. Feel the weight of your bed covers, the temperature of your body, and the temperature around you. Notice the rhythm of your heartbeat. Listen to the sound of your breathing. Feel the air entering your lungs. Notice how your stomach expands each time you fill it with air.

Acknowledge any tension in your body. Visualize it rising to the surface of your body and let it go.

There are so many things you can be aware of right now. Being mindful and present brings your focus away from your busy mind.

Focusing on your breathing is the simplest and easiest way to relax your body and mind. Noticing that you are focusing on your breathing also has relaxing effects.

When thoughts arise in your mind, just notice them and let go. Bring awareness back to your body and maintain your focus on your breathing. Keep breathing in and breathing out, noticing the air going in and out through your nose.

It will help you easily and naturally calm, relax, and fall asleep.

Now I invite you to visualize. You can do it with your eyes opened or closed. It's up to you.

Imagine your mind as a spinning wheel. It spins around at a fast speed. Now, allow it to slow down, more and more.

It's now turning slowly; it's barely moving. Time has slowed down. Your thoughts have slowed with it. You are relaxed now. Your mind is calm.

Your eyes are now tired of watching the wheel. They need a rest. Now, push the image further and further, like in a small motion. Push it further until it's just a distant dot.

Now, see yourself lying on the grass under a huge tree with a green crown. You work as a shepherd. It's a lazy, warm afternoon. The evening is coming, and the sun is setting. You need to collect your sheep before the day is done. They are all over the pasture. You know that you have fifty sheep. So, you start counting sheep and collecting them across the field. One, two, three, four, five, six, seven, eight, nine, ten, eleven, twelve... Count further, until all of your sheep are collected together. Take them to the cote for sleep.

You are tired, and you lie on the grass again. You're snuggling in a warm and comfortable sleep bag. You are going to sleep outdoor, under the night sky, full of stars. You gaze at stars, thinking about how many children will be born all around the world this night. How many people will start their lives while these stars are in the sky? You start choosing names for those children and giving names to the stars by them.

The first one is Jake, and the second one is Julie, the third one is George, the fourth is Joanah, the fifth is Michael, the sixth is Rachael, the seventh is Methew, the eighth is Helen, the ninth is Alex, the tenth is Tracy... and so on. You made up ten names. Then ten more. You give names to stars and children that are going to be born until you feel so tired that you can't think of anything anymore. You doze off and fall to deep, deep sleep. You will stay asleep the whole night, and, when you wake up in the morning, you will feel great, full of energy for a new day.

Guided Meditation for Overcoming Depression

Welcome to the meditation for overcoming depression.

The effects of meditation on healing depression have been researched, and the techniques used in this meditation are evidence-based. You can use it whenever you need a relief of sour feelings. Using it daily will tremendously help you overcome depression.

Your mind has created a habit of feeling bad and producing chemicals that make you feel that way. What you need to do is to reverse the process and create the habit of feeling good, so your brain starts producing feeling-good chemicals again. It won't happen overnight, but if you do whatever it takes to overcome the devastating feeling, it will pay off tremendously. This meditation will help you to train your mind to feel good again and to start building a new habit and producing feel-good chemicals. So, in this meditation, the goal is to feel good. That's the only thing you need to do. If you feel like you're lying to yourself, don't worry. That's because you are breaking a habit of negative thinking, and your mind is showing resistance. You'll build a new habit, a habit of feeling good, and it will help you reverse the cycle and change the mindset. As building a new habit requires a long time, try to practice this meditation every day or every night while you sleep. Meanwhile, start taking little steps towards a better life in your daily life. Start doing things that make you feel good. Start small, and you'll build a joyful and happy life.

Now, make yourself comfortable. First, we'll relax. Take a deep breath in and breathe out. Prepare yourself for relaxation.

Breathe in, to the count of four. One, two, three, four.

Breathe out, to the count to six, while relaxing your feet. One, two, three, four, five, six.

Take another breath, counting to four. One, two, three, four.

Release the breath, counting to six, and relaxing your lower legs. One, two, three, four, five, six.

Inhale, to the count of four - one, two, three, four.

Exhale, to the count of six, relaxing your thighs. One, two, three, four, five, six.

Take a deep breath, to the count of four.

Breathe out, relaxing your glutes, hips, and pelvic area, to the count of six.

Count to four while you are inhaling again.

Exhaling, relax your fingers and palms, while counting to six.

Take another breath, to the count of four.

Breathe out, counting to six, and relax your forearms.

Inhale to the count of four, and then exhale, counting to six and relaxing your elbows.

Breathe in, to the count of four.

Breathe out, to the count of six, and relax your upper arms.

Take a breath, to the count of four, expanding your stomach.

Exhale, to the count of six, and notice your belly contracts. Allow it to relax.

Breathe in, counting to four.

Breathe out, to the count of six, and let your chest relax.

Take another deep breath, to the count of four.

Releasing it, count to six, and let your back relax. Repeat it once again. Relax the whole back.

Now breathe in, again, to the count of four.

Breathe out, counting to six, and relax your neck and throat.

Breathe in - one, two, three, four.

Breathe out and relax your scalp - one, two, three, four, five, six.

Inhale, to the count of four. One, two, three, four.

Exhale, counting to six, and relax your facial muscles. One, two, three, four, five, six. Relax your jaw, your lips, your cheeks, your eye muscles, your eyebrows, and your forehead.

Pay attention to thoughts in your mind. Take a deep breath in and release the breath, allowing them to disappear along with the breath. Release everything you don't need anymore. Let them fade away and disappear. Let your mind slow down. Now, pay attention to the thoughts remaining in your mind. Let them slow down. Take a deep breath again. While breathing out, release your remaining thoughts again. Your mind is clear and relaxed. You are feeling better. Tell yourself: I feel good. I don't need a reason to feel good.

Breathe in, breathe out. Tell yourself mentally: I feel great.

Breathe in and breathe out.

Bring attention to your body, and notice any tension in it. Allow that tension collect at one point as you're inhaling. Exhaling, let it out. Release all the tension along with the breath. Let it go. As you release tension, you feel even better. Breathe in and breathe out. Tell yourself again: I feel good.

Focus on any pain hiding in your body. Take a deep breath in, and breathing out, let go of all the pain. You don't need pain. Allow yourself to feel good. Tell yourself: I feel great.

Do you feel any suffering in the body? It might be old suffering or from the present. Bring it to the surface as you're inhaling. Exhaling, release all the suffering along with the breath. Let it go. Allow yourself to feel good.

Your body is relaxed. Your mind is clear and calm. You feel great right now.

Notice the connection between your body and mind. They work together and feel together. Feel and see that connection. Visualize your brain producing chemicals that make you feel great. Feel amazing. Feel those vibrations from your mind making you feel wonderful in every part of your body. Visualize and see those signals from your brain spreading through the whole body.

Breathe in, breathe out.

Repeat to yourself: I feel good. I feel amazing.

Your subconscious mind can't tell the difference between true and false. It believes in anything you tell it. Now, you are feeding your subconscious mind with positivity, building new thinking patterns that will work for your highest good. Feel the pulses coming from your brain, going through the whole body, spreading wonderful emotions. Enjoy these sensations and feelings. Notice positive emotions becoming stronger and yourself feeling better and better. You deserve to feel good; you don't need any reasons for that. Take some time for yourself, to feel great for no reason. The positive feelings in the body become stronger. Allow yourself to enjoy it. Breathe in, breathe out. Repeat to yourself: I feel good. I feel amazing. I enjoy this moment.

Try to recall all the things you are grateful for, big or small. Focus on all your blessings now, everything that brings you joy, people who bring happiness into your life, and all the joy you bring to others. Feel gratitude, and enjoy this beautiful emotion for as long as you wish. Your subconscious is soaking in this amazing feeling. So much good is happening in your body and mind right now.

As you sink into a relaxing slumber, enjoy those affirmations:

I feel so good.

I am full of joy.

I am full of happiness.

I am full of love.

I love myself.

I am grateful.

I am strong.

I see the good in everything and everyone.

I am complete and enough.

I deserve to feel good.

I am full of energy.

My life is meaningful.

I create a better life for myself and my loved ones.

I am full of gratefulness.

I am thankful for all the amazing people in my life.

Thank you.

I feel so good.

I am full of joy.

I am full of happiness.

I am full of love.

I love myself.

I am grateful.

I am strong.

I see the good in everything and everyone.

I am complete and enough.

I deserve to feel good.

I am full of energy.

My life is meaningful.

I create a better life for myself and my loved ones.

I am full of gratefulness.

I am thankful for all the amazing people in my life.

Thank you. Thank you. Thank you.

Guided Meditation for Overcoming Depression 2

Welcome to the meditation for getting out of depression.

People who don't understand what's happening when one suffers from depression often think it's the same as being sad or unmotivated. They might even advise you just to shake it off or deal with it. But the truth is quite different. We all have tough days from time to time. But, when suffering from depression, every day feels horrible. Nothing is fulfilling anymore, as the whole world has lost its colors.

In this meditation, I'll try to bring back some light into your life. We'll work on seeing the positive sides of things. It might be hard when your own brain is playing tricks on you. But with everyday practice and consistency, you can train your brain to produce substances that make you feel good again.

Take a deep breath, counting to four. One, two, three, four.

Breathe out, counting to eight. One, two, three, four, five, six, seven, eight.

Again, breathe in and count one, two, three, four.

Breathe out, counting: one, two, three, four, five, six, seven, eight.

Now, breathe in and hold your breath to the count of three - three, two, one. Breathe out, saying to yourself, "relax."

Again, breathe in, hold - three, two, one, and breathe out and "relax."

You can relax now; you are in a safe place.

Is there any tense spot in your body? Notice them. It might be your neck, your shoulder, your toes, or jaw. Do you feel nervous, like butterflies in your stomach? Relax those parts. Scan your whole body, from toes to the top of your head, and notice where do you hold tension in your body. Focus on those parts, allowing them to lose and relax.

Perhaps some thoughts are going through your mind. Let them go. Thoughts are just thoughts - you don't have to follow them. They can do nothing to you; they have no power, nor importance. Allow yourself to let them pass by.

Your mind is playing tricks on you. While you are trying to reverse the cycle and see the good side of things, it's used to focus only on negativity. It requires some time to rewire it and train it to work properly again. It is a matter of brain chemistry, but you can do a lot to take back control over your mind.

Now, visualize, you are sitting in a chair in an empty room. You have your stuff packed in suitcases and waiting for a cab to pick you up. You are leaving for a journey.

Now, waiting for a cab to come, use your time to close your eyes and think about things and circumstances that have affected you recently and brought you here. How does your current life look like? What made you lose your old self?

Take a moment to congratulate yourself for seeing things for what they are. It's a huge step towards your healing.

Imagine you are opening your eyes. It all has sense now. You can see the present clearly, without shifting to the future and the past all the time. You are aware there are things you need to let go. Sometimes we need to let things go so we could move on.

The cab is here. You are picking your luggage and closing the front door. The driver takes your suitcases and put them in the trunk. He opens the door for you, and you're sitting on the backseat. While the cab is driving down the street, you look from the window. You can see your life for what it is. You clearly see everything you don't like in your current life. Everything is greyish, and nothing excites you. You think about how you really need a break from that all. When you come back, your perspective will be different.

The cab is entering the train station. The kind driver is smiling, wishing you a nice holiday. The cab is leaving the station, and you stay waiting for your train.

The train is here. You get on and find your compartment. You are the only one here. Have a seat and make yourself comfortable for a long ride. The train is leaving the station. You look out the window. The world outside looks different now. You can see green, trees and fields, hills, and mountains in the distance. The further you get, the more different things look. You are thinking about possibilities and changes. Everything can change, and there are almost limitless possibilities. The grey and plane sightseen became green and alive. Life is a constant change.

You start to doze off, and your eyes feel sleepy. Have a nap if you want. There's nothing else you should be doing right now. You have enough time to rest.

The train slows down, and you can hear the bell is ringing. It has arrived at the station. You step off the train and see your new driver. He smiles and holds the table with your name on it. You sit in the luxurious limousine. The seat is soft and comfortable. You feel safe in this new cab. From the window, you can see the world out there. It's colorful and vibrant.

You see the sign for the airport. The cab stops. You are at an airport for private jets. Your kind driver helps you get on the plane. Have a seat and make yourself comfortable. The pilot and a stewardess greet you smiling. You feel welcomed and relaxed. The airplane leaves the ground and flies up into the air. As it goes higher, you feel more and more positive. The ground disappears from sight. You have left everything behind. This is the break you deserve. Relax in the chair. This is a comfort zone, and nothing bad can happen. Take a nap if you want to.

The flight is almost ended. The plane is landing. You have arrived at your destination.

Looking from a cab, you can notice this is a completely different place, and everything is different. The world out there looks colorful, joyful, vibrant, welcoming. You feel excited to explore it. You enjoy feeling the warm breeze from the opened window of the cab.

You've reached the destination now. You'll stay in a beach cottage. The beach is beautiful, with white sand, and the sea like a melted turquoise. You enter the cottage. Everything feels relaxing here. You can hear the waves rolling on the beach. You open the white door and take off your shoes. You step barefoot on the beach. It feels so relaxing to walk along the beach, feeling the white sand and cool water through your toes. For a long time now, you didn't feel so relaxed. It's like being yourself again.

The sun starts to set. The sky looks magnificent. You are now sitting on the sand, looking around. You notice many things around you - threes in the distance, seagulls, waves, rocks, sparks of the setting sun on the water.

You begin to feel relaxing tired.

You walk back to the cottage. There's a queen-sized bed with a comfy mattress and white sheets. You have left all the worries behind. You feel peace and serenity. You're lying your head down on the pillow and falling asleep. Your muscles are relaxed and heavy. Your mind is clear. Your emotions are light as feathers. You drift off into a deep slumber.

When you wake up, you'll remember this journey and the sense of tranquility.

Guided Mindfulness Meditation for Overcoming Anxiety

Welcome to the guided meditation for overcoming anxiety using mindfulness. Being mindful means being consciously present in a moment, and aware of everything that's going on within you and around you.

Anxiety is a common issue these days. It's not pleasant at all. Perhaps you feel like you are in danger most of the time, although there's nothing that endangers you. Your mind is doing its best to protect you, turning on the „fight or flight" mode, preparing your body to run or fight. But, since there is no real need for that, this state of mind and body does more harm than good for you. You need to find a way to tell your mind, „It's okay; we are safe; you don't need to protect me so hard." The way to say it so your brain can understand you is to calm down your breathing and body. That way, you'll turn off the „fight or flight" button, and eventually, your mind will calm down, giving up from overprotecting you.

Anxiety is often caused by constant racing of our minds. You should know that you are not alone in this—many people all around the world search for ways to cope with anxiety. Mindfulness can tremendously help here. Since anxiety is a consequence of being mentally too much in the future, bringing awareness to here and now can make a world of difference. Being mindful means finding that golden point of awareness and being completely present.

By choosing to take time to practice meditation and learn how to be more mindful, you have already made the first step towards overcoming anxiety.

During this meditation, we'll calm and slow your breathing, focus on physical sensations, relax the whole body, and be consciously present for a while. Focusing on physical sensations will ground you and help you getting out of your head and calming your busy mind while relaxation will help you get out of fight or flight mode.

I invite you to find some quiet place and make yourself comfortable. Experiencing ease in your body will help you feel the same for your mind. You can sit on a floor, on a chair, or lye, whichever you like. Make sure that your clothes are comfortable, that all tight pieces of clothes or belts are loosened, and you are not too warm or too cold. If you want to practice this meditation before sleep, get ready for bed as you usually do.

Focus on my voice. I will guide you through this experience. We'll try to achieve complete awareness and presence. I suggest you do this meditation with your eyes gently open. You can close them later during the meditation, but try to stay alert.

Focus your vision on a particular point in front of you. Narrow your focus on that point and allow everything else to fade away into the background.

Now, slowly broaden your field of view and allow the background to come into your eye vision. With awareness, notice everything you can see. Don't turn your head; just look consciously at everything in your view. What colors can you see? Try not to name them or judge if you like them or not. Just notice the colors, their shades, the textures, materials. Notice all the tiny details you wouldn't notice otherwise.

Our breathing is so simple yet the most powerful way to ground ourselves in the present.

Bring attention to your breathing. Notice the natural depth and rhythm of your breathing. Don't try to change it, for now, just notice. Listen to the sound of your breathing. Now, look for any movement in your body connected to breathing.

Now, intentionally begin to deepen your inhale and slow down your exhale.

Breathe in through your nose, counting to four. One, two, three, four.

Then breathe out, also through the nose, counting to six. One, two, three, four, five, six.

Repeat it a few times. Inhale. One, two, three, four.

Exhale – one, two, three, four, five, six.

Breathing that way, with exhales longer than inhales, will relax you and tell your mind everything's okay. You are safe. You don't need to run away nor to fight. You can rest and relax.

Take time to notice all there is to experience about your breath.

Focus on those still moments, pauses between every two breaths. Feel the air filling your body and leaving it. Feel its way, from your nostrils, all the way to your lungs, and back outside.

Once again, breathe in – one, two, three, four. And breathe out – one, two, three, four, five, six.

If your regular breathing is too shallow or deeper than that, or can't reach those numbers, don't force it. Just try to breathe out a bit longer than you breathe in.

There are certainly some thoughts going through your mind. Don't stress yourself about it. Your mind is used to be busy. Just let them pass. Imagine your thoughts and worries as colorful balloons flying away. As your breathing is slowing down, your mind is slowing down, too. There are fewer balloons there, and they fly slower and slower.

With special attention, notice pauses between each breath and a similar pause between your thoughts. Mentally link those two. Allow yourself to be in this gap between every two breaths and thoughts. Allow your attention to rest in this space. If your thoughts are still wandering, and you tend to follow them, come back to your breath and the gap between breaths.

Now, broaden your awareness of physical experience.

Bring attention to your body. Feel the points of touch with the surface below you. You might feel the line of connection blurred, or you might experience it as warmth or pressure. Feel your feet on the surface, or your back on the surface of the chair. If you are lying, feel the all touching surface – your back, the backside of your legs and arms, the back of your head. Feel the texture of the surface, its temperature. Is it a cold, smooth floor, or a soft bed covers, your favorite chair, or a cushion you're sitting on, feel it.

Be aware of any sense that you can smell. Focus on scents you can feel.

Then bring your attention to sounds. What can you hear? Perhaps you can listen to some sounds from the outside – traffic, birds, voices. Or some constant sounds of appliances in the home. Hear the sound of your breathing. Acknowledge the rhythm of your heartbeat. Notice the details in the sounds you are hearing. There are always many sounds around us; it's just a matter of focus if we will acknowledge them.

Bring your attention to the surface of your body, your skin. Be aware of everything that touches your skin. Feel the brush of your clothes, the touch of your bed shits, or covers if you are lying.

Feel the temperature of the space you are in.

Take a deep breath, filling your stomach. Exhale as slowly as you can.

Spend some time simply being. Be aware of everything within you and around you. Feel the beat of your heart and the flow of your blood within you.

Bring awareness to your body. Try to feel the aliveness in all the parts of it. Nothing can ground you at this moment better than awareness of sensations in your body.

Take a deep breath, taking the air deeply, so your stomach expands like a balloon.

Breathin out, focus on your hands, fingers, and palms. Feel aliveness in those areas. Simply be aware of all the sensations in this part. You may feel it as warmth or tingling. If you feel the urge to move your fingers or hands, allow yourself to do it. Feel the movement, be aware of every sensation.

Bring awareness to your arms. Notice everything you can feel on and within them, from wrists to your shoulders. Feel the touch with the surface on the backside. Feel the temperature of the air around on your skin. Being so aware of a particular body part means you are already relaxing that part.

Bring awareness to your toes and feet. Feel the tingling in your toes, the relaxed feeling in your feet. Then allow this relaxed feeling to spread up to your ankles, your inner legs, your knees, and upper legs. Focus on all the sensations in your whole legs – warmth, the point of touch between the surface and your skin. Acknowledge the sense of relaxation in your hips, glutes, and pelvic area.

Then continue, moving your awareness up, to your stomach and chest. Be aware of your stomach moving up and down in the rhythm of your breathing. Feel the air expanding your stomach and chest, and leaving it with the exhale.

Breathe in, to the count of four. One, two, three, four. Breathe out, to the count of six. One, two, three, four, five, six.

Repeat it a few times, focusing your undivided attention to the way of the air in through your nose, to the lungs, and your stomach, and all the way back.

Put special attention on still periods between every two segments of breathing. Feel grounded, and allow yourself to sink deeper into the surface.

If any thought arises, just imagine it like a colorful balloon and let it fly by. Resist the impulse to follow it. Just stay outside of it and observe it. You are not your thoughts. Your thoughts have no power over you. Acknowledge they're just that – thoughts, products of your mind.

Continue gradually moving this relaxed scan of your body. Bring awareness to your back. Feel the surface above it. Focus on sensations in your back muscles. Scan them by your awareness, one by one, starting from the lowest point. Feel the heaviness and warmth in your back muscles and your spine. If you can feel any tension remain in your back, give some special attention to that point until you feel it melting and releasing.

Bring awareness to your neck. Feel the weight of the head it holds. Acknowledge all the sensations in your throat.

Bring awareness to the crown of your head. How often are you aware of it? It's time to give it your attention. If you have hair, feel the touch of it on your head. Take a breath in and imagine you are inhaling pure peace. Allow it to spread through your head, relaxing all the muscles.

Focus on each muscle on your face, one by one. Scan them with your awareness. Become aware of any sensation in your eyes and your mouth. You can close your eyes if you want.

Take a few deep breaths again. With each inhale, imagine you are breathing in peace, tranquility, and relaxation. With exhale, let go of everything that doesn't serve your peace of mind and body. Imagine you are breathing out all the tension, and feel your body getting softer, heavier, and relaxed. Let it sink into the surface beneath you, completely supported.

Feel the temperature of the air around you. Feel it with your palms, your lips, your forehead, your lower legs.

What can you hear now? Try to count all the sounds you can listen to at the moment. Focus on each of them for a while. Imagine them entering your ears.

If there is any area of your body that is not relaxed yet, give it special attention. It is trying to tell you something. Sometimes, giving special attention to some sensation in our body is enough to make it soften and fade away. Bring your attention to the areas of your body that are telling you something. Notice the sensation and stay with it for some time. If your mind is drifting to overthinking or old patterns of thinking, gently come back and stay with the experience of the sensation.

Take a deep breath. Exhale slowly. Each inhale is bringing you peace and healing.

Every exhale takes away everything you need to let go of.

Every moment is so beneficial for you.

Imagine what's going on within your body now – your organs, your muscles, your bones, your nervous system – all of that is feeling your peace and are relaxing. Now you are giving them time to heal and recharge. This is healing for you.

Inhale peace. Exhale anxiety.

Inhale tranquility. Exhale tension.

Inhale calmness. Exhale rush.

You are present and aware now. This is how it looks like to be mindful. This moment is the only reality that exists for you. There's no such thing as the past or the future. If you have any worries lingering in some corner of the mind, imagine it as a balloon you're holding. Open your hand and let it fly away. If you still have more worries bothering you, imagine you are holding a bunch of balloons. Let them all fly into the sky. You are the only one who is holding them here. You don't need them anymore. Worries are just a way your mind is playing tricks on you. You don't have to follow them nor to engage. Whenever you notice that you are about to lose yourself in your thoughts, bring your attention back to your breathing, surrounding, and your physical sensations.

When you are completely aware, grounded in the present, anxiety can't survive. It must fly away with all the colorful balloons you are letting go of.

Take another full breath again. Fill your stomach and your chest with peace and calmness. Breathe out as slowly as you can, letting go of each and every remaining piece of anxiety, tension, and busy mind.

Listen to these affirmations and repeat them mentally or out loud:

I'm aware of my breathing. I'm aware of the air going in and out of my body.

I'm aware of my body. I'm aware of my heart rhythm.

I'm aware of my fears and anxiety. I'm aware of the discomfort I feel.

I'm aware of the negative thoughts that make me feel anxious.

Now, I'm slowly calming my mind.

I'm calming my anxiety.

I'm relaxing my body and slowing down my thoughts.

I'm letting go of negative thoughts.

I'm letting go of fears and concerns.

Each moment, I'm finding more peace.

I am safe.

Being aware of my breathing, I'm letting go of everything I don't need anymore.

I inhale serenity.

Everything is just the way it should be.

Everything's happening for my higher good.

I am divinely protected and guided.

Everything happens when the time is right.

Whatever I need comes to me.

Whatever I should know, reveals to me.

I am calm and relaxed.

I am in peace with the world.

I am in peace with life.

The world is a safe place for me.

I am powerful.

I am strong.

I am present and grounded.

I am in perfect balance.

I inhale calmness. I exhale peace.

While breathing, smile at yourself.

I am safe and secure. I give myself permission to be in peace.

I'm well.

Things are getting better and better every day.

I expect great things to happen.

I accept my anxiety. It's just trying to protect me. Thank you. But, I don't need you anymore. I am safe now, and I am letting you go.

Feel the lightness.

I accept all of my emotions and allow myself to experience them.

They don't define me. I can watch them while remaining calm.

I'm healing all the time.

My body and mind are in a healthy harmony.

I allow myself to be in peace.

I feel born again.

I feel wellness in the whole body, in each cell of my body.

I am full of energy.

I allow myself to rest in this comfort and peace.

I enjoy this tranquility and gentleness.

I enjoy being in this completely relaxed state, free from anxiety.

You can start over with your aware presence as many times as you need.

In your usual life outside the meditation, look for patterns and situations when you might be rushing. Then intentionally slow down and come back to experience life fully. When we try to control life, and we constantly rush, we can't experience it fully. On the contrary, when we slow down and stay with our sensations, we can notice more, experience more, live more fully, and savor life. So, allow yourself to slow down and rest in the gap between thoughts. When you quiet the noise in your head, you are able to see, hear, and feel everything around you, you are aware and open to life.

When you feel ready, gently open your eyes, stretch yourself, get up, and move on with your daily activities.

Guided Meditation For Overcoming Depression

Welcome. This meditation is aimed to help you with depression and depressive moods.

You'll be keeping your focus on your breath and learn how to look at your thoughts and feelings in a new way.

You may feel more hopeful immediately, as soon as you finish the meditation. With repeated use, you may notice that you feel depressed less frequently, until, one day, you realize that you are your old self again.

You can do this meditation anytime and anywhere. However, it's best to choose a time when you know you can have some undisturbed quiet time, and it's safe to close your eyes and relax.

For the beginning, find a comfortable place and position. You may lye or sit on a cushion with your legs folded in front of you or sit upwards on a chair. It's up to you, and everything is okay as long as your back is straight.

Make sure that your clothes are comfortable, loosen all the restrictive pieces or belts. Turn off any ringers and notifications.

Place hands on your lap, palms up, or on your knees. If you are lying, let them straighten from your body.

If possible, close your eyes. If you can't do it, or it's not convenient, don't worry.

Take a few deep breaths. Breathe deep and slowly. Connect with your breath. Feel the air entering your nostrils. Notice the movement of your belly with the in-breath and out-breath.

Now let go of controlling your breathing and allow it to settle in its natural rhythm.

Pay attention to sensations in the whole body. Be aware of your postures; feel all the parts of the body.

Continue to breathe in your natural pattern.

Depression is universal; it's part of being a human. It affects everything - out body, the way we think and feel, all the life fields. There's a whole package of negative feelings coming with depression. Your way of thinking is negative, you can't see anything positive, and you may lose any interest for life. Depression is a natural reaction to loss. But you can be depressed with no apparent reason, too. That doesn't mean anything's wrong with you. Either way, your thoughts, and emotions are normal. However, despite it's not enjoyable at all, depression can bring you some good, too - It can make you look inward, focus on problems and search for solutions or reevaluate things in your life and make adjustments.

We all get depressed from time to time. But too much depression, which lasts for too long isn't healthy. It has the ability to perpetuate, making you depressed for longer than you should be.

Fortunately, there is a solution. There are techniques that help in coping with depression, and you can learn them. This meditation will help you with it.

You shouldn't suppress, ignore, nor deny your emotions and thoughts. If you fight them, they'll grow and get stronger. Nor you have to figure out where they came from and why. None of these will get you to the root of your problem. Instead of trying to get rid of your unlovable thoughts and emotions, it's wiser to change your relationship with them. Instead of suppressing and fighting hard feelings, you'll make space for them, accept them, and give them your attention. You'll see, much to your surprise, how they lose their power and fade away.

Find a comfortable posture, so that you can relax, but yet stay alert.

Breathe in your natural pattern. You don't need to change your rhythm nor depth of breathing for now. Just breathe in your usual way. Place your attention to the nose. Feel the air entering your nostrils. Feel its coolness. Now, notice the air leaving your nostrils, notice its warmth. Do this for a few moments. Focus on breathing the fresh air in, and breathing warm air out. Concentrate only on sensations in your nose.

Do it once again—cool air in, warm air out.

Now, explore your breath and allow yourself to experience it fully. Watch your breath, be curious. Have the experience of breathing and observe yourself having it at the same time.

If your natural breathing is long and deep, notice that. If your normal breathing is short and shallow, notice that, too, without judgment. If the way your breathing changes or stays the same, notice that. Don't try to change or fix anything. Don't hold for beliefs of "how things should be." Instead, accept the things for what they are and just observe without trying to control.

So, we are still observing your natural breathing pattern.

Sooner or later, you will lose your focus. It's perfectly normal, so don't criticize or judge yourself. We all get distracted, and focusing requires some practice.

Distractions always come from one of these sources - your thoughts, senses, or feelings. When a distraction occurs, just notice it and let go. Then gently bring your focus back to your breath. Try to do it for a moment, with the next distraction. Notice, and let go. No need to push it away. Don't fight it, don't suppress it, just let it float by.

Whenever your mind begins to wander, notice what's going on. Bring your attention back to your nose, sensations in it, breathing in and out.

It's also expected to feel the urge to name a distraction. For instance, you may mentally say "alarm is ringing in the next apartment," "kids are making noise outside," "traffic," "dog's barking," or so, whatever distracted you. Try to name just one thing instead, more general and more in connection with what's happening with you - "distracting" or "wandering," for instance. Bring your attention back to your breathing. Try this for a moment, with the next distraction or mind wandering.

Now, the next time you lose your focus, try not to name things internally at all. Just notice that you have lost your focus and bring it back. Try this with the next distraction.

Most likely, depressive thoughts and feelings will intrude. Those are ones you are trying to escape from. The trick is to learn to bring your attention back to your breathing instead of following those thoughts. Breathe in your natural way. When a negative thought arises, just notice it and let it pass by. It will be easier each time because you already know how to let thoughts go. Gently bring your focus back to your nose and your breathing. Try it for a moment. Notice the negative thought occurring. Let it float by you, easily, without pushing.

When you feel depressed, your mind constantly rushes in the future or stays stuck in the past. Staying in the present, on the other hand, and focusing on your breath and sensations in your body, helps you stay balanced. When you focus on breathing, you are grounded in the present. Try to stay present with each moment of your next few breaths. Feel the air entering your nostrils. Feel its coolness. Follow its path to your lungs and belly. Notice movements connected with breath. Feel all the sensation it provokes in your body. Follow its way back, and feel the warm air leaving your nostrils. Do this, be intentionally present, and completely aware of every moment of your next few breaths.

You will most likely be distracted by negative feelings, too. They go hand in hand with depressive thoughts. You'll probably experience some of these - sadness, emptiness, anxiety, anger, rage. Emotions are nothing else but a combination of your thoughts and sensations in your body. Acknowledge that and mentally divide a negative emotion into those two parts. Feel the sense it provokes in your body. You might feel it as an ache in different body parts, tension in your head or neck, a weight on your chest, fatigue, monotony. Allow yourself to experience what you feel, without need to change it, solve it, taking any action about it.

The second part is to see the thoughts in your mind. Acknowledge the connection between those two. Your thoughts provoke your body to feel a certain way, and you experience those two together as an emotion.

Make a conscious choice to place your attention on the sensation in your body, not the thought. Rest your attention on the sensation. Notice if it's intensity changes or stays the same. It might happen to disappear under your focused attention.

Now, leave the emotion and the sensation in the body and gently bring your attention back to the breathing and the way it feels in your nose. Breathe in and feel the cool air entering your nose. Breathe out, and focus on the warmth of the air that's leaving your nose.

If you choose to follow your distressing thoughts, it will make the negative feeling stronger. But, if you choose to pay undivided attention to the negative sensations it provokes in your body, depressive and distressing thoughts diminish. They need your negative thoughts and their stories to feed themselves. If you focus instead only on your physical sensations, negative emotions can't survive, and they fade away, bringing you relief.

Notice that focusing on your breathing and physical sensation grounds you in the present and brings you relief better than anything else.

Now, visualize you are at a train station. People are rushing in all directions. There are the hustle and bustle all around you. You are standing still on your platform, waiting for your train. The world around you seems dull and grey—colorless people in their grey suits, dirty streets around the station, grey station, and ugly trains. You are wearing a plain, grey pelerine with no defined shape. You are also carrying a heavy bag, made from dark leather. It's so heavy that your arms sore. But you can't put it down. You have to carry it wherever you go.

Thoughts may come and go in their rhythm while you are observing the world around you. Don't worry- all the mental chatter will pass; just let the thoughts be and be gentle with yourself. People and your thoughts are passing you by in their busy manner, but you remain completely calm. You know you will be leaving this hectic environment in a moment, as soon as your train arrives. Think of this moment as an escape that will help you think clearly again. The train will take you to a far destination, where you feel peaceful and calm. You know you'll come back as a different person. You are ready to begin the journey.

Your train arrives, and you are stepping abroad. Give yourself permission to devote this time to yourself, to spend some time alone, to relax. You know you'll gain a new perspective, and you also know that this has to be don. So, don't feel guilty. You find your carriage. It's empty, and you are the only passenger here. Take a seat and finally put your heavy beg down. It's such a relief! Your muscles automatically relax. The sense of tranquility fills your mind and body.

The voices from the station start to fade away. You are looking through a window. That's the same dull and grey world out there, but you can observe it from a distance now. You are leaving it behind now, and it's natural to feel sadness and regret, or relief, knowing that you are leaving everything that was holding you back.

Take this me-time to rest and relax. Allow yourself to see your needs and desires. Your sadness is trying to tell you something. Perhaps it's trying to show you that you have neglected your needs and needs of your soul. It suffers and uses unpleasant feelings to gain your attention. You have enough time to relax the whole body.

You've created a distance now, and you can see your life from another perspective. From your window, the world outside looks different now. The sky looks more blue and clear, the grass and trees are greener.

The further you get from the train station, the easier you feel. Your feel calm and positive. Your arms and hands are rested from heavy baggage. Your muscles are relaxed in a comfortable seat. Your breathing is deep and slow. Your stomach is quiet and steady. Your legs and feet are comfortable and relaxed. Your mind slows down to a pleasant speed. You feel free to just be yourself, in balance, and let everything just be as it is.

Reaching your destination, the train stops. You pick up your heavy, black bag, and step off the train. You have just a few more streets to walk to your special place.

The bag is too heavy, but you know it will be over soon. You feel stronger now, determined, and enthusiastic.

Here you are, in front of a large gate. You open it with effort. You are in your private garden. It's been a long time since you were here last time. It looks neglected. No one was taking care of it while you were occupied with your sadness and pain. You step on the path that leads through the garden. There are no flowers, nor grass. Where there were weeds, there are no flowers. You go to an old tree on the backside of the garden. There's a spade recumbent to the tree. You are taking it and starting to dig. You are digging a hole in the shade of the tree. Once the digging is done, you open the bag, curious to find out what was the heavy baggage you carried around. On your surprise, the bag is full of your worries, your fears, sadness, anger, and regrets. You can see them as large, heavy stones. It's time to bury them. Visualize you are taking the rocks, one by one, and drop in the hole. Name your stones by your hard feelings and mentally say to each of them while laying it into the ground "I'm letting you go."

Let go of sadness.

Let go of regrets.

Let go of anger.

Let go of self-doubt.

Let go of resentment.

Let go of bitterness.

Let go of monotony.

Let go of hatred.

Let go of jealousy.

Let go of misery.

Let go of helplessness.

Let go of hopelessness.

Let go of fears.

Let go of the pain.

Let go of suffering.

Let go of everything that makes you feel bad.

Do this as long as you need to bury all of the stones from your bag. In the end, bury the bag, too. Bury the hole and feel the relief.

Go back to an old bench in the middle of the garden. Take a seat and enjoy the feeling of ease and freedom. Feel the lightness. Notice the sun is shining through the trees. Look around. Nurturing this garden will need just a little energy, to fix everything and bring its old glow. Taking care of this place is the priority now. You'll enjoy every moment of it and the results.

Rest deeply in your garden, imaging its final look, when you take care of everything. Inhale the sunlight. Exhale peace. Look colorful flowers. Smell the roses. Feel the enthusiasm. Realize that your journey brought you here to remind you of who you really are. Your old self is back. Smile to who you really are. Enjoy watching the dance of light and shadows in your garden, and mentally say to yourself:

I am free.

I am relaxed.

I am peaceful.

I am grateful.

I am light.

I am happy.

I am energetic.

I am full of love.

I am calm.

I am safe.

I am powerful.

I am joyful.

Life is good.

Life is colorful.

Life is magnificent.

I love myself.

I know my value.

I appreciate myself.

I accept myself.

I love life.

I am free.

I am relaxed.

I am peaceful.

I am grateful.

I am light.

I am happy.

I am energetic.

I am full of love.

I am calm.

I am safe.

I am powerful.

I am joyful.

Life is good.

Life is colorful.

Life is magnificent.

I love myself.

I know my value.

I appreciate myself.

I accept myself.

I love life.

Breathe deeply and smile to yourself with every exhale.

Enjoy for a while in this relaxed state, feeling warm sunlight on your skin. You can take this feeling with yourself.

When you come back from this trip to your usual daily life, you will have a completely different perspective.

Your private garden will always be there for you, and you can come back whenever you wish.

When you feel ready, gently open your eyes and go on with your usual daily activities. Or, you can drift off to sleep and have a relaxing, deep rest.

Guided Meditation For Stress Relief

This is a meditation for stress relief. Stress is so common these days that we don't even notice how stressed out we are. Stress is not always a bad thing. It helps us stay alert and productive, to strive for our goals and achievements. However, when stress becomes chronic, it is exhausting. It drains our energy and negatively impacts all the life fields, especially our health. That's why we need to take time for relaxation and stress relief intentionally.

Imagine I am here, with you, to help you lower your stress level, calm, and alleviate that burden.

You can use this meditation or particular techniques applied here whenever you want - when you feel stressed and tensed, before or after a stressful event.

Choose a quiet and comfortable place and time in the day when you won't be disturbed. Turn off all distractions and consciously dedicate this time to your well-being. You deserve it. Everybody deserves to decompress and relax. Our natural state is relaxed and in ease. We are just taught to be stressed all the time. Your mind and body need some time to process experiences, rest, recharge and heal itself. Stress doesn't allow them to do that.

To help stress relief, we'll focus on three levels - your breathing, your body, and your mind. Our goal is to slow down and deepen your breathing, to relax your body completely, and to calm your mind.

Know that it's okay to have thoughts, it's expected during meditation, and don't stress about it.

Allow yourself o simply be there. Let go of any expectations and judgment. Focus on this very moment and be open to whatever it brings you.

Elongate your spine, if you are in sitting position, make sure your back is straight, yet not tensed. If you are in lying position, make sure your spine is straight, yet relaxed. Take a comfortable, effortless position and gently close your eyes.

Invite your attention inward, to your breathing. Notice the path your breath takes as it travels through your body. Feel the air entering your nostrils and travels through your nose, down to the lungs, and expanding your stomach. Then feel the sensations as it leaves your stomach, your lungs, traveling back out through your nose. It's so simple, yet most important connection between us and life. Notice all the movements in your body connected with breathing. There's always so much going on in our bodies even when it seems we do nothing. Notice the sensations in the body that breath provokes, and how it makes your body feel.

Now, try to deepen your breath by counting. Breathe in, to the count of four. One, two, three, four.

Hold the breath to the count of three. One, two, three.

Breathe out, to the count of six. One, two, three, four, five, six.

Repeat it once again.

Inhale - one, two, three, four.

Hold - one, two, three.

Exhale - one, two, three, four, five, six.

Now, while breathing in, visualize that you are collecting all the stress from your body.

Breathe out slowly, as if you were blowing a dandelion. Let go of all the stress with the breath.

Once again, mentally collect all the stress and tension remaining in your body, and blow it out.

With the next breath, visualize, you are breathing in peace and tranquility. Allow it to fill your stomach and lungs. Slowly breathe out, mentally saying to yourself: relax.

Once again, take a deep breath, inhale peace, and relaxation. Exhale slowly, repeating: relax.

Enjoy this deep, relaxed, and slow breathing. When thoughts appear, just notice and let them float by, gently bringing your focus back to the path of your breath through the body and the sensations it provokes.

This mindful attention and breath awareness is a practice for quickly reducing stress and relaxing. You can use it whenever and wherever you need it. Your breath will always be with you, for as long as you live.

Stress affects our body on so many levels. It interferes with the blood flow, heart rhythm, work of all our organs and cells. Our mind suffers, even our skin. Our magnificent bodies have the power to heal themselves. However, when we are stressed, it becomes impossible. It's like holding a poison within us. That's why it is tremendously beneficial for us to learn how to release stress and practice it regularly.

It's crucial to relax the body so you could relax the mind, too. Now, I invite you to tense up your body and then relax it, part by part.

Turn your awareness to your toes. Take a breath and tense up the whole feet. Hold the breath and the tensed muscles counting three, two, one. And release. Breathe out and relax the feet.

With the next breath, tense up your lower legs and knees. Hold it - three, two, one. And relax.

Take another deep breath and tense your upper legs and hips as tight as you can. Hold your breath - three, two, one. And release the tightness with exhaling.

Now, with an inhale, tighten your glutes. Hold it tight for a moment. Three, two, one. And exhale, relaxing the muscles.

Now, breathe in and clench your fists. Hold it to the count of three - three, two, one. Breathe out, and allow your fingers and hands to loosen and relax. Relax your palms, and allow them to open against the ceiling. Relax your wrists.

Inhale, and tighten your lower arms and elbows. Feel the tightness in your upper arms. Hold the breath for a moment. Three, two, one, and release tension. Feel the all muscles in your arms loosen and relax.

With the next breath in, tense up your shoulders and lift them up so they can almost touch your ears. Hold the breath - three, two, one. Breathe out and relax your shoulders. Let them loosen and drop down.

Our shoulders are often the place where we hold most of our burden - all the stress, worries, tension. Let it all drop from your shoulders now. Take a breath, and with the exhale, let all the weight fall from you.

Now, contract your abdominal muscles as tightly as you can. Pull them to your spine to feel the tension. Hold for a moment—three, two, one, and release. Relax your stomach and allow it to turn into its natural rhythm of moving with your breath.

With the next breath, fill your lungs and tense up your chest. Hold to the count of three, two, one. Breathe out, relaxing your chest. Feel your ribcage is floating, relaxed.

Stretch the muscles of your back. Feel the tension in the back and your spine. Hold the breath - three, two, one. Breathe out, relaxing all the back muscles, one by one.

Repeat this for the lower back, for the middle, and the upper back.

Inhale, tense the muscles of your lower back. Hold - three, two, one. Breathe out, and relax your lower back muscles.

With the nest breath, feel the tension in the middle part of your back. With the exhale, relax those muscles.

Tighten your upper back muscles. Hold for three, two, one. And relax.

Stretch your neck and tense it while breathing in. Hold the breath - three, two, one. Release the breath and relax your neck.

With the next breath, feel the tension in your scalp. Stay with the sensation for three, two, one. Breathe out and allow your scalp to relax.

Feel the intense tension in your forehead. This part is often too tensed due to overthinking. Tense it even more by raising your eyebrows. Hold it tensed for three, two, one. Then release. Breathe out and relax your forehead, allowing all the tension to drift away.

Breathe in and squeeze your eyes, tensing all the tiny eye muscles. Hold it tight for three, two, one. Then, breathe out and relax your eyes. Loosen all the muscles around them and allow your eyes to sink into the head.

Clench your teeth and the jaw with the next breath. Hold it to three, two, one. Breathe out and release. Allow your jaw drop, so your teeth aren't touching. Relax your lips and release tension in your tongue base.

Now your whole body is relaxed. Scan it mentally once again. If you feel tension anywhere, make a conscious choice, and put the intentional effort into relaxing that area.

If there is any stress remaining in any corner of your body, allow it to collect on the surface, from where it will disappear with your breathing out.

Since the tensed body is a consequence of a stressed mind, a relaxed body is sending signals to your mind to relax. Everything is fine. You are safe. You are relaxed and powerful. All the stress has drifted away.

Now, when your breathing is deep and slow, and your body is completely relaxed, it's time for your mind to calm and relax.

That is where most of our stress is produced. We are used to creating numerous thoughts and follow most of them. So, our minds are overwhelmed by the burden, all sorts of worries, fears, to-do lists, and scenarios of what might happen. In a constant rush, our minds have o time to slow down and relax. Most of health issues and conditions come from the mind. That's why it is crucial to learn how to soothe our minds and give them time to repair and recharge. Even the best personal assistants, as your brain is, need rest.

Accept the fact that there will always be some thoughts going through your mind. It's perfectly normal, and it's the mind's job to produce them. So, don't stress yourself about that.

Take a deep breath. Notice the first thought that is arising in your mind. Don't engage, don't follow it. Just notice it, and with breathing out, let it go.

Repeat this with the next one. Notice the thought forming in your mind. Take a deep breath. Exhale, and let it go.

Notice how thoughts are slowing down to accommodate the rhythm of your breathing.

Some of the thoughts are fast, like bouncing balls. Catch it, and hit it as far as you can. Some of them are a bit slower, like a big beach ball. Some of them are slow and floating, like balloons. Catch them gently just for a moment, and let float by. As you are going on with this practice, breathing, noticing, and letting go, you'll notice that your thoughts became slower and lighter. There will be less of bouncing balls, and more of balloons. Moreover, they will come to you so easy like soap balloons or feathers. Notice the feather floating to you. Just blow it away and watch it pass by.

You can also visualize every hard thought, everything that causes you stress, as a dark cloud. Imagine you are lying and watching the sky. For every dark thought, imagine a small, dark cloud in the sky. Give them different shades of the dark - from greyish to black, depending on how stressful the thought is.

Once you are done with sending your worries and stress to the sky, it's time for relief. Watch your stressful thought and the dark cloud you created for it. Breathe in, and with breathing out, imagine you are releasing all the stress. While doing it, watch how all the darkness is leaving the cloud. It is changing the color, becoming lighter and lighter, until it is white and fluffy.

Skip to the next one. Breathe in, collecting all the stress and darkness. Breathe out, let go, and watch the cloud becoming snow white.

With the next breath, take up all the darkness from the next thought and cloud and breathe it out.

Do this for a while, until all the clouds become white, light, and feathery. Feel ease. Enjoy the sensation of being free from stressful thoughts. They are not hard nor dark anymore. Your burden became lighter and easier.

Now, take a deep breath, and breathing out, imagine you are blowing the first white cloud away. It flows away and disappears in the distance. There's clear blue now in the place where it used to be. Breathe in, and repeat with the next cloud. Breathe out and blow it away.

Do this for all the clouds.

There is a clear, blue sky with no clouds above you now. Your mind is clear, too. Enjoy this sense of calmness, easiness, and lightness. Your mind is relaxed now.

With your mind relaxed and calm, go back to focusing on your breathing.

With each breath, mentally say these affirmations to yourself:

I am calm. Breathe out.

Breathe in through your nose. I am relaxed. Breathe out through your mouth.

Breathe in. I feel ease. Breathe out slowly.

I feel tranquility.

I am confident.

I am skilled.

I am focused.

Breathe in and say to yourself: I can handle anything that life brings to me. Breathe out.

There is peace within me.

Breathe in through your nose. I feel relaxed. Breathe out through your mouth.

I am intelligent.

I am calm.

I am wonderful.

I am relaxed now.

Take a deep breath. I make peace with everything outside and within me. Breathe out slowly.

I feel all the cells of my body are relaxed now.

I bring light and ease with me wherever I go.

I am powerful.

I can handle everything with ease.

Breathe in through your nose. I am in harmony. Breathe out.

I am calm. Breathe out.

Breathe in through your nose. I am relaxed. Breathe out through your mouth.

Breathe in. I feel ease. Breathe out slowly.

I feel tranquility.

I am confident.

I am skilled.

I am focused.

Breathe in and say to yourself: I can handle anything that life brings to me. Breathe out.

There is peace within me.

Breathe in through your nose. I feel relaxed. Breathe out through your mouth.

I am intelligent.

I am calm.

I am wonderful.

I am relaxed now.

Take a deep breath. I make peace with everything outside and within me. Breathe out slowly.

I feel all the cells of my body are relaxed now.

I bring light and ease with me wherever I go.

I am powerful.

I can handle everything with ease.

Breathe in through your nose. I am in harmony. Breathe out.

Feel your body relaxed from head to toes. Feel the surface comfortably supporting you. Visualize a cloud forming beneath you. It's the size of your body, and it's the most comfortable place you've ever been to. It's supporting you perfectly, cradling your relaxed body, soft yet secure. Rest on this cloud. It's here only for you.

Now, feel the cloud slowly moves up. It elevates, taking you further and further from the ground. You know you are safe and secure, and you can rest on your cloud, even so high in the sky.

You can see the land. Everything seems so small from here. You can see places, mountains, rivers, fields. Everything seems like a colorful quilt. Now, look at all those things that used to provoke your stress. It's surprising how small and insignificant they look like from here! All the troubles, worries, issues with health or finances, everything that bothered and stressed you out is left down there, and you can barely see it. Here, on your fluffy cloud, you feel no stress and have no worries: just relaxation and the feeling and ease.

Now, imagine a golden light suddenly starts to shine from the center of your cloud. It looks like a little Sun is hidden behind it. The light becomes stronger and stronger, and now the whole cloud shines brightly. You can feel the light is penetrating your body and spreading through it. Your feet glow, your whole legs shine. You can feel your stomach and chest shine with golden light. Your hands and arms also glow. Now your head is radiating the light. Your whole body shines. You can feel the light spreading on the inside, too, filling your heart and making your blood golden, too. The light is healing and relaxing. It's a cure for any stress. As you radiate it, you spread peace and calmness. It's everywhere, within and around you. It wraps and covers you, relaxing your thoughts, emotions, your cells, organs, bones. It lights up any darkness and stress remaining anywhere within you. Have a bath in the golden light and enjoy resting in it. All the stress seems like a distant memory. You don't have to turn back to it ever again. You will always have this feeling to come back to. You can get on your cloud and rest in golden light, far away from everything that stresses you out.

You are completely relaxed now. All the stress is drained out of you. Your breathing is deep and slow, your mind is clear and calm, and your body is completely relaxed. Your cloud is back on the ground now. You can get up from it when you feel ready.

Gently open your eyes, and get back to your usual activity, completely renew and stress-free.

Guided Meditation For Overcoming Insomnia

Good evening. Welcome to the guided meditation, which is aimed to help you overcome insomnia. If you have problems with falling asleep or staying asleep during the night, this meditation is for you. You can use it whether you often have trouble sleeping or just from time to time. It's not pleasant at all to lie sleepless and feel exhausted the next day, unable to afford a quality rest to your body and mind.

Use this meditation before sleep as a part of your evening routine. Prepare yourself for bed in your usual way, lie, and find the most comfortable position. The temperature should also be pleasant, not too warm, nor cold. You can lie on your back or on the side, whatever best helps you to relax. I invite you to listen to my voice. It will guide you, help you relax, and take you to a calm, calm state from which you can easily fall asleep.

Words in this meditation will talk to your conscious and subconscious mind. That way, it will help you easily fall asleep and stay asleep for the whole night. Finally, you'll have a recharging, restful sleep. The first time since long ago, you won't wake up during the night, and you'll finally feel rested and refreshed in the morning.

This might not happen the first few times you do this meditation. What will undoubtedly happen is that you will relax more and be feel less tensed. Good night sleep is a habit. To build a habit of easily falling asleep and staying asleep during the night, you will need some time and practice. But it's established, it will pay off in levels of energy and life satisfaction. So it's worth a try. We recommend you be patient and consistent in using this meditation every night before sleep. It will undoubtedly lead to forming better sleep habits and eventually overcoming insomnia.

The first time you fall asleep in moments and stay asleep until the morning comes, wake up renewed and fresh, you'll realize that all the efforts have paid off, and this was the best thing you could do for yourself.

We often have hard times trying to relax and fall asleep because our minds refuse to calm and stop thinking. When our bodies calm down to rest, our brain seems to find it the best time to go into overdrive. If you are one of the people who overthink, especially when it's time for sleep, you can't stop mentally repeating, and it would be best to write it all down. That way, you'll put it aside for later, without worry that you might forget something important, and you'll free up space in your mind, allowing it to calm down. So, pause the meditation and download it all from your mind to the paper. Your actions and concerns can wait. Now it is time for rest.

I invite you to put your attention to my voice and ground yourself in this very moment. Feel the comfort and the warmth of your bed. Feel the ease because it is time when you don't need to do anything. This is time only for you, and your reenergizing. You don't have to do a thing. Just listen to my voice without any expectation nor insisting on falling asleep. Even if you stay awake all night long, this meditation will bring you relaxation and rest. So don't put any pressure on yourself. All you need to do is lying in your bed, listening to the words, and relaxing. If sleep comes, great. If not, not a big deal, it's okay, too. You will rest anyway.

Take a deep breath in, to the count of four. Hold the breath to the count of three. Breathe out, as slowly as you can, counting to six.

Repeat it a few more times. Take a deep breath in, to the count of four. Hold the breath to the count of three. Breathe out, as slowly as you can, counting to six.

Do it once again - take a breath, one, two, three, four. Hold it, one, two, three. Exhale, one, two, three, four, five, six.

And, one more time - breathe in deeply, counting to four. Hold breath the count of three. Then, breathe out, counting to six.

If you can't reach these numbers, it's okay, too. Don't force yourself; do what you can. Then, allow your breathing to fall into its usual rhythm.

With each breath out, allow your body to relax a bit more and sink deeper into the surface.

Now, see your thoughts come and go. They do it all the time. Your busy mind is used to produce them all the time. But you don't have to follow each of them. It may be such a precious insight – you are not your thoughts. Even more, you are always choosing which of them you want to think. They are just products of your mind, and you are the one who decides. So, if you're going to rest your busy mind and fall asleep, let your thoughts float by, like little clouds or soap bubbles. Since you can't forbid your mind to do its job and create thoughts, the only thing you can do is to remove your focus from them. Focus on something else, and unwanted thoughts will lose their power and diminish. Eventually, your mind will slow down and stop creating them. That's why mindful focus on your breathing, physical sensations, and environment can do a long way to relax and calm a busy mind.

First, bring your awareness to your body and its sensations. That is the first step towards mindful presence.

Notice how your body feels. Acknowledge its posture, feel the temperature of your body and space around. Feel the support of the surface below you and the comfort of your mattress. Feel the weight of your body, and the weights of bed covers. Feel your heartbeat and notice the rhythm of your blood flow. Focus on your breathing and listen to its sound. Place your attention on your nose. Feel the air entering your nostrils and going down to fill your lungs. Fill the stomach with the air and allow it to inflate like a balloon. Then follow the way of the breath back, notice how it leaves your stomach, your lungs, and finally, your nostrils. Notice the coolness of the air you are inhaling, and the warmth of it on the exhale when it went throughout your body. Focus only on your breathing and movement and sensations it provokes in your body. It is the easiest and quickest way to ground yourself and relax.

How do your feet feel? How do your legs feel? Notice sensations in each part of the body. How your glutes and the pelvic area feel? What do you feel in your stomach? How does your back feel? Notice all the sensations in your fingers, hands, and arms. Acknowledge how your shoulders and neck feel. Then bring your awareness to sensations in your head and face. If there is any tension in your body, acknowledge it. Allow all the tension arise from all the deep or hidden corners of your body, coming up to the surface. When you feel that all the tension is collected on your skin, let it go.

Take a deep breath, and with exhale, let go of tension.

Repeat this a few times until you feel your body is completely relaxed, free from any tension.

Do a quick scan of the whole body, part by part, checking if all the parts are relaxed.

If you find any tension, simply let it go with breathing out.

There are so many things you can place your focus on right now. Even the busiest mind calms when you are mindful and truly present.

Sooner or later, your focus will drift off from your breathing and physical sensations. Gently bring them back. Concentrating on the feelings in your body and your breathing is the simplest yet most powerful way to stay present and grounded, calm, and relax.

Thoughts will eventually appear in your mind. Don't stress about it. Notice them, and let go. Do it as many times as needed, always bringing your focus back to your breath and your body. Notice the air entering your nose, and stay with the breath throughout the body, moment by moment. That is a natural way to calm and, after some time, drift off to sleep.

Breathe in, breathe out, and with a smile, greet the feeling of relaxation and letting go. This is time only for you. This is time to recharge and gaining fresh energy. Stretch your body and feel how comfortable it is to lie in your bed, having nothing else to do. The night is meant for having rest from everyone and everything, even our thoughts. With every breath, dive deeper into the sense of comfort and relaxation.

Visualize, you are in a kanu boat, on calm, clear water. The boat is floating in the place, cradling you gently. Listen to the sounds of water. Your eyes are closed, the sun is shining, tenderly to your skin. Your boat is incredibly comfortable, soft like a cloud, yet strong enough to support you. You are safe and calm.

Feel the joy and the ease of the moment. It's beautiful. Breathe in, breathe out, and smile to yourself.

The boat is large enough for your whole body to lie comfortably. It's time for you to relax the whole body, part by part, by scanning it with your mindful attention, healing light, and your inner smile. Relax your toes and feet. Allow them gently open to the ceiling. Relax all the muscles of your legs. Relax your lower and upper legs, and knees. Relax your hips and pelvic area. Relax your glutes and notice how the whole lower part of the body is relaxed. Allow your fingers to relax, and your palms opened up to the ceiling. Relax your wrists, and whole hands and arms.

Place your inner smile into your belly. Feel the calmness and peace in your stomach. Allow it to move easily in the rhythm of your breathing. Notice how relaxed it is. Relax your chest, and feel them floating.

Now, relax your back, from the lowest point, up to your neck. Relax your vertebras, one by one, and feel each muscle loose and relax, becoming soft, like during a massage. Breathe in, and breathe out, visualizing you are exhaling through your spine everything you want to let go.

Our shoulders are the most crucial point in relaxation. That's where we hold and carry most of the weight, all our worries, fears, and hard feelings. Most of us go through life, not noticing our shoulders are tensed and tight. Relax your shoulders now. Let go of all the weight and let them drop from the ears.

Relax your neck, allowing it to lose and soften, leaving your head cradled by the soft pillow. Open up your throat and allow all the muscles there to relax.

Our central, the head, is often overwhelmed. Let it relax. Relax your scalp and the forehead. Relax your eyebrows and all the tiny muscles around your eyes. Allow your eyes to rest and sink into the head. They work hard all day long. It's time for them to finally have a proper rest. Relax your cheeks and your lips. Release your jaw and allow the base of your tongue to relax. Relax your ears and intentionally release any tension you might be still feeling anywhere in your head and face.

Once again, do a quick scan of the whole body, to check if it is completely relaxed.

Your feet – relaxed. Your legs, knees, upper legs – relaxed. Your hips and pelvis – relaxed—your glutes-relaxed. Your hands – relaxed. Your arms, elbows, and upper arms – relaxed. Your belly – relaxed and calm. Your chest – relaxed. Your back, from the bottom to the top – relaxed. Your shoulders and your neck – relaxed. The top and the back of your head – relaxed. Your face – relaxed. Your eye muscles, your nose, your cheeks, your mouth, your jaw – all relaxed.

Now, when all the parts of the body are relaxed, it's time to pay attention to your skin and allow it to relax, too. It works all the time, protecting your body from the outside world, and it needs rest and reenergizing.

Visualize the other organs in your body. Take a moment to appreciate everything they do for you all the time. Smile at them with your inner smile, send them love and light, and allow them to relax. Imagine your body on the inside. Imagine your organs working for you all the time. Mentally send them love and let them relax.

Acknowledge that your emotional part needs rest, too. Emotions are turned on all the time, but you don't need them right now. Give your emotions permission to let go. Forgive everything there is to be forgiven. Let go of all negative feelings. The only thing you need now is inner peace and tranquility. Don't hold andy anger, resentment, nor sadness. Let go of everything that doesn't serve you.

If any thoughts occur, and they certainly do, let them pass you by. You don't need any of them right now. It is not time to think or solve problems, to be productive, nor to achieve anything. It is time to rest your mind. Let it recharge now so you could be productive when the time for that comes.

Visualize you are in a dark, empty room. The only thing you can see is a clock on the wall. The clock hands are moving in the speed of your thoughts. The only thing you should do is counting the movements of the clock hands. You find it harder and harder, because they move slower and slower, while you are becoming more and more sleepy. You notice they become slower and slower until they are barely moving. Your mind is calm and clear now, and you are just a step away from drifting off to sleep.

Observe your body becoming heavier and sleepier. You are in a state of deep relaxation now. Watch your slow and deep breathing, your calm mind, and a relaxed body. There's no urge to change anything. There's only calm, mindful observing and acceptance. You feel the warmth, the coziness, the peace, and deep calmness. Everything's calm, peaceful, and easy. Everything you don't need fades away into the blurry background. Inhale. Exhale. This is how it feels to be relaxed on a deeper level.

You are carefree. All is well. Breathe in, breathe out.

Let go of all of your concerns, all the fears, and worries. Everything will be just fine. Everything happens when the time is perfect. Leave everything to higher intelligence, and trust all will be well.

Enjoy the serenity and carefreeness, giving up of control and allow a dream to come.

This is a moment of perfect balance and harmony.

Notice your deep, calm breathing. Feel comfort and ease, becoming one with the moment, giving up any effort. Your body and mind are enjoying these moments of absolute rest.

You are in a forest, high in the mountains. The sun is shining through the trees. You've been hiking in the hills the whole day long. You feel pretty tired now. But your house is still quite far. So you have to walk about an hour more until you get there. You know that a fire in the fireplace, a cozy blanket, and a warm, comfortable bed are waiting for you.

You're stepping down a steep, narrow path. You feel so tired that you start to count your steps to move attention from your soring feet. You are walking and breathing deeply fresh mountain air, counting your breaths out. Breathe in. Breathe out. One. Breathe in. Breathe out, two. Inhale, exhale, three. Breathe in, breathe out, four. Breathe in, breathe out, five.

Your feet are tired. Your legs are sleepy. Your back needs rest. Your mind is sluggish. Your eyes are struggling to stay open. Your hands already sleep. You are yawning, wishing only one thing – to get to the house soon and sink in the bed. You're going down the steep path. You know you have to get there before the day ends. You can hear birds and insects in the grass, your steps down the path, and the sound of your breathing.

You are still breathing deeply, counting on your exhales. The night is about to come. The forest is preparing for sleep. It becomes harder and harder to walk and to count as you become more and more sleepy. You wish to lie down the tree and just allow yourself to fall asleep.

You are yawning and barely can walk. Fortunately, just a few more steps, and you'll get to the small house where you finally can sleep. The Moon and stars appear in the sky. You finally reached your destination. You're opening the wooden door. Your legs are heavy, and you can barely move. The fire is crackling in the fireplace. You are lying on the cozy bed, placing your head onto a soft, fluffy pillow, wrapping yourself in a warm blanket.

You can feel your legs are already sleeping. Your stomach is sleeping. Your back is sleeping. Your head and face are sleeping. Your whole body is sleeping. It's now time to allow your mind to fall asleep, too.

Mentally repeat those statements:

I am calm.

I am peaceful.

I am tranquil.

I am free.

I am worth everything life has to give me.

I am full of love.

I am healing.

I am recharging.

I am re-energizing.

I am resting.

I am divinely supported and guided.

I am safe.

I am secure.

I feel good.

I feel comfortable.

I feel light.

I feel serene.

Everything's all right.

I'm free to rest now.

While you are falling asleep, acknowledge that all is well. You'll have a good, quality night rest. You'll fall asleep now, and stay asleep during the whole night. In the morning, you'll wake up refreshed and renewed.

Feel the serenity. Feel the calmness. Feel the tranquility and deep peace. Allow yourself to sink into a deeper sleep, knowing everything is fine. You are calm. You are safe. You are worthy. You deserve good rest.

Step into the sleeping state where the problems of the day are solved. Good night, and have

nice sleep.

Guided Meditation For Self-healing

Welcome. This guided meditation is aimed to help you to activate your abilities to heal yourself. Whether you have some severe health issues or you just don't feel very well, using this meditation will help you. You'll feel better immediately after finishing it, and, after some time of everyday use, even serious illness might disappear, or you can see unbelievable improvement in your health.

There is a power within you that can heal even from worst conditions. That is the same divine power that has created you. Our bodies have the ability to repair themselves and to achieve perfect balance. When we are not in balance, illnesses may occur. The process works in the opposite direction as well, so if you manage to bring back perfect harmony, health issues disappear.

However, to heal themselves, your body and mind need some peace and quiet time. If you are in a constant rush, always active, tensed, never completely relaxed and tranquil, your body can't repair itself. That's why meditation is the perfect way to enable self-healing. Your body has its own wisdom, and you don't need to teach it anything. You just need to move from the way and allow it to do its job. Your busy mind is the one who needs to be calmed so the natural processes can go on undisturbedly.

In this meditation, we'll do all that is needed to remind your body of how to heal itself, and everything to allow it to do that. You will learn how to relax the whole body, calm mind, slow and deepen breathing, show appreciation, and love to your body, and remind it of its natural powers.

You can do this meditation whenever you like, during day or night. For the best results, I recommend you do it as often as possible. Find a quiet place where you won't be disturbed for about an hour. This is the time only for you and your healing. Make it a priority. Turn off any ringers, all notifications, and all distractors. Choose the most comfortable position. I recommend practicing it in a lying position, but choose whatever is most convenient. For the best experience, use earphones.

Place your attention to my voice. It will guide you to a deeper, relaxed state from which you can empower your body to heal itself, and engage in your healing process.

Make yourself comfortable. The temperature should be pleasant, not too warm, nor cold. Your back should be straight, your legs straight, slightly apart, and hands straight beside your body. Slowly calm before the meditation begins.

Try to calm and slow your breathing. Exhales longer than inhales are the sign for your body to relax. Breathe in through the nose, to the count of four. One, two, three, four. Breathe out through the mouth to the count of eight. One, two, three, four, five, six, seven, eight.

Repeat it. Breathe in. One, two, three, four. Breathe out. One, two, three, four, five, six, seven, eight.

Do it once again. Inhale - one, two, three, four.

Exhale - one, two, three, four, five, six, seven, eight.

If you can't reach those numbers, don't worry. Do what you can without forcing yourself.

Being gentle to yourself is now a priority.

Now, allow your breathing to drop back to its natural rhythm.

With every breath in, imagine you are inhaling white, healing light. With each exhale, let go of everything you want to let go. Negative emotions are like a poison inside you. Let them go.

Inhale white light.

Exhale tension.
Inhale light. Exhale anger.
Inhale light. Exhale anxiety.
Inhale healing. Exhale resentment.
Inhale light. Exhale hatred.
Do this for a while, until you let go of all negativity you've been holding inside.

It's time to relax your body now. From the relaxed state, you can talk to your body, send it love and appreciation, and help it activate its natural healing power. When you relax completely, you move your consciousness from the way, and your body is free to repair.

Breathing slowly and deeply, bring your attention to your toes and feet. Feel the aliveness in them. Tense your feet, and then allow them to loosen. Relax the whole feet, from toes to heels. Relax your ankles. Tense the muscles of your lower legs. Hold them tensed for a moment. Three, two, one, and relax. Relax your knees. Place your focus on your thighs. Feel the backside of your thighs on the surface. Tense the muscles of your thighs. Hold it for three, two, one, and relax. Allow your legs to open up a bit to the ceiling. Tense your glutes as tight as you can. Hold for a moment, three, two, one, and relax. Allow your glutes, hips, and pelvic area to relax. Take a breath in, and breathing out, relax your lower body a bit more. Do it a few times. Feel the relaxation and ease spreading through your lower body, and it becomes heavier, sinking in the surface.

Your hands are lying straight beside your body, with your palms up. Feel the aliveness in them. Bring your attention to the sensations in your fingers. Stretch and tense them for a moment, and then relax. Relax your palms, hands, and wrists. Move your attention up to your forearms. Tense them to the count of three, two, one, and then relax. Relax your elbows. Move up to your upper arms. Tense the muscles, and hold them tight for a moment. Then allow them to loosen. Your whole hands and arms are relaxed, from very fingertips to your shoulders.

Notice the movements of your stomach, as it moves up and down in the rhythm of your breathing. Pull your navel to the spine and tense the abdominals. Hold them tight for three, two, one. And relax.

Take a nice, deep breath, fill your chest, and tense them. Breathe out, and allow your chest muscles to loosen. Feel the relaxed feeling in your stomach and chest.

Bring your awareness to your back. Feel the surface below, supporting it. Tense all of your back muscles. Breathe in, and with the breath out, relax your lower back. Inhale deeply again, and exhale, relaxing the middle part of your back. Move your attention up, and with the next exhale, relax your upper back. Feel your back is loosened and relax, sinking into the surface. Feel the lightness, as you were floating yet been strongly supported.

Now, tense your shoulders as firmly as you can, so they can almost touch your ears. Then, with the exhale, allow them to drop and relax. Feel the muscles of your shoulders loosen and become soft and elastic. With each exhale, your shoulders become more and more relaxed. With your shoulders relaxing, the whole body becomes relaxed. Feel the relief, calmness, and peace in your body.

Tense your neck by pushing your jaw to your chest. Then bring your head back and relax your neck. Bring your awareness to your throat. With the next exhale, allow your throat to relax and open. Clench your jaw. Then release it, allowing it to drop down. Tense your facial muscles, and then relax them, one by one. Relax your cheeks, the eye muscles, your lips, and tongue. Raise your eyebrows and tense the forehead and the scalp. With breath out, allow them to relax. Relax the back and the top of your head. Feel its weight, and your head being cradled by the surface.

Your whole body is completely relaxed now. Feel the ease and tranquility. Breathe deeply and slowly, and enjoy these moments of deep relaxation. Your organs, systems, your blood, bones, and cells are relaxing now. They are all regenerating and healing. There's so much happening within your body right now. Appreciate those moments of deep reenergizing rest.

How often do you tell your body how thankful you are for everything it does for you? It is time to let it know how grateful you are.

Mentally say „thank you" to your feet and legs for holding you and taking you wherever you want to go. It's such a blessing to be able to walk and change places. Thank your glutes for supporting you while you are sitting. Thank your genitals and reproductive organs for bringing you joy and possibilities to reproduce yourself. Thank your urinary and digestive systems for cleaning your body and getting rid of everything you don't need anymore. Mentally say thank you to your stomach for digesting food for you, enabling you to use nutrients. Show appreciation to your lungs for making you breathe and use the air, which keeps you alive. Thank your back for supporting you, holding you up and straight. Say „thank you" to your hands for doing so many things for you - for holding, bringing, carrying, hugging, creating, and so much more they do for you. Thank your neck for holding and moving your head. Too often, we don't notice these „workers" within our body, and we are not aware of how blessed we are to be able to move, to breathe, to walk, to see. Acknowledge your blessings. Thank your brain for doing such a magnificent job of thinking for you and managing all the activities within your body. It's such a great manager! Thank your mouth for enabling you to express yourself, to communicate, to feel the taste of the food you eat, to kiss those you love. Say „thank you" to your nose and to your eyes. It's a precious gift being able to see. You can see colors, the faces, the stars glowing in the dark. Feel appreciation so deep to fill the whole of your being. If you count all of your blessings, it's not surprising even if you begin to cry from happiness and gratefulness.

There's no better cure in the world than love. Love can heal everything. So, show your body how much you love it. Pour love in each part of it.

Again, start from your feet. Mentally say them, „I love you." Move up, sending your love to your legs, your hips, glutes. Feel the love for your belly and chest. Your back also needs to hear, „I love you." Pour love into your hands and arms. Say „I love you" to your shoulders and neck. Then, pour love into your head. Mentally say to your body, „I love you. You are great. You can do amazing things. I pour love in every part of you." Pour love in every organ, every muscle, and bone. Pour so much love in each cell as it can hold, so every cell of your body becomes a tiny star that spreads the love around. Your body is full of love now. Your organs work cheerfully—your blood flows in the cheerful rhythm. You are bathing in self-love. It cures everything. It repairs, rejuvenates, and heals everything that needed to be fixed. If there is some part of your body that needs your special attention, pour some extra love in that place. The infinite and unconditional love is spreading from your heart.

You are in a state of deep relaxation. Your breathing is slow and deep. Your body is full of divine, infinite love that is healing it. From this point, you can talk to it, to empower the process of self-healing.

Remind your body of its natural power to heal itself and restore balance, and show it your trust.

You can mentally repeat or just listen to what I am saying.

Body, I love you. You are perfect, just the way you are.

I pour love into you.

You deserve to be perfectly healthy.

You are meant to be balanced and work as a wholeness.

Health is your inborn right.

You are wise.

You have the ability to heal yourself, and you know how to do that.

I trust you and encourage you to do that.

I allow you to do whatever it takes to heal.

You don't need help, just my trust, and support, and I am giving it to you now.

I allow the divine power within you to guide me and to bring you back to your natural state of harmony.

I listen to you, I understand you and appreciate what you have to tell me. Now, I know you do that because you need my attention.

I let go of everything that stands on the way to healing.

I'm ready to let go of any negative emotions, limiting beliefs, and holding stubbornly to anything. You know the best what's best for you.

You know the way, and I trust you.

Heal yourself, heal every cell, and every organ within you, make everything do in a perfect way, because I love you, you are amazing, and you deserve to be healthy and happy.

I know you have everything you need for healing, and you will do that perfectly in a way that is best for you.

Now, visualize, you are in front of a massive, golden gate. You push it, and the door opens. You are stepping into a beautiful garden. It's full of green; there are high trees, flowers, and grass. It's silent, and you can hear only birds and insects. The sunlight is shining through the crowns. As you are stepping down the path, you can hear the sound of water. You still can't see any water, but you can hear it. So, you move on down the path in the direction from where the sound is coming.

This garden is huge. Finally, in front of you, there's a marble pergola. That's where the sound is coming from. Coming closer, you can see a pool there. The water is crystal clear, sparkling. You know that is healing water, that helps the body to remind of its self-healing power. You sit on the side of the pool, with your feet in the water. On your surprise, your feet start shining. You decide to get into the water. It's only waist-deep at this side of the pool. You're looking at your legs, and you can see they are glimmering. The feeling is as if the water is massaging your feet, legs, and hips. With each step forward, it's a bit deeper. You are moving on, enjoying the feeling, and knowing that healing is happening right now. Finally, you dive in and feel the water wrapping you. It's above your head, and your whole body is sparkling with glimmering shine.

Getting out the water, you feel renewed and refreshed as if it washed off everything you needed to shake off.

Your body is reminded of its powers and abilities to heal. It's full of energy and strength. You know the healing process is already going on.

Besides the pergola, there's an outdoor daybed with canopy. You didn't notice it at first. You know it's here for you. So, you lye down and make yourself comfortable. You can feel a soft breeze on your skin and the comfort of the mattress. You can hear the water sound and feel the smell of fresh grass.

Your whole body is relaxed, rejuvenated, and full of fresh energy. You breathe deeply, knowing a new part of the healing process is about to begin.

Take a deep breath in and imagine a healing, golden light entering your feet. With the breath out, notice your feet are shining brightly.

Breathe in and feel the light entering your muscles and bones of your lower legs. Breathe out, and visualize your legs shining with golden light. Breathe the light in your upper legs, allowing it to fill your thighs and hips. Your hips and whole legs are shining with golden light. On the inhale, fill the light entering your pelvic area, and on the exhale, see the bright light radiating from your glutes and pelvis. Breathe the healing light filling your stomach. Breathing out, see the bright light spreading from your center.

Inhale the healing light and fill your chest. Exhale, and feel your chest shining.

Breathe the golden light through your spine and allow it to spread all over your back. The golden light is entering every muscle of your back. Breathe out. Your back is shining. It seems as if you are lying on the shiny star.

Breathing in, imagine the light entering your fingers and spreading through your hands. The golden light is filling your lower and upper arms. Breathing out, notice your arms and hands shining gold.

The golden light is moving up to your shoulders, and they shine. With the next breath in, your neck and head are filling with the healing, golden light. Exhaling, notice your head is shining brightly.

The light is entering through your skin, wrapping your organs, penetrating all bones, and muscle tissues. Your cells are shining, bathing in golden, healing light.

While your body is healing, bathing in golden light, using divine wisdom and its natural powers to heal, you can empower it by sending love, blessings, and positive, supportive thoughts. To build perfect health and achieve balance, you need to adopt new thinking patterns. You can repeat those affirmations mentally or out loud. They will become your new beliefs and help you create a supportive environment for healing.

I have the power to heal.

I am strong and powerful.

My body and mind are healing now.

I deserve to be perfectly healthy. That is my natural right.

I am ready to forgive and let go.

Life is supporting me.

The Universe is holding my back.

I love myself, unconditionally.

I choose health.

I am full of energy.

All of my cells are healthy and vibrant.

I am grateful for my body and its wisdom.

I am thankful for my positive, healthy thoughts.

I am grateful for the perfect balance of my body and mind.

I am complete.

I am whole.

I feel great and full of energy.

I allow my body and mind to heal.

I love life, and life loves me. It has a lot to give me, and I am ready to experience it.

I am in perfect harmony and in peace with the world. I allow divine energy and higher intelligence to guide my body and heal it.

Take a nice, deep breath. Breathe out slowly.

When ready, gently open your eyes. You can move on with your day, feeling fresh and reenergized. Or, if you want, let yourself drift off to sleep, and have nice dreams.

Guided Meditations for Deep Sleep, Relaxation, and Stress Relief:

Bedtime Stories for Adults, Hypnosis & Beginners Meditations for Insomnia, Self-Healing, Depression

Contents

Sleep Meditation (30mns) 1
Deep Sleep Meditation (60mns) 6
Sleep talkdown 1 (10mns) 15
Sleep talkdown 2 (10mns) 17
Deep Relaxation Guided Meditation (30mns) 19
Stress Relieving Morning Meditation (20mns) 25
Post Work Stress Relieving Meditation (20mns) 29
Anxiety Meditation (15mns) 31
Meditation for Reducing Anxiety (30mns) 33
Meditation for Managing Panic Attacks (30mns) 40
Relaxation Meditation (15mns) 44
Depression Relieving Meditation (30mns) 47
Pre-Sleep Stress Reduction Meditation (15mns) 52
Insomnia Meditation (20mns) 54
Deep Sleep Meditation (30mns) 57
Sleep Hypnosis 1 (90mns) 62
Sleep Hypnosis 2 (90mns) 71
Bedtime Stories for Adults 1 (90mns) 76
END OF MEDITATIONS 89

Sleep Meditation (30mns)

Hello and welcome to this meditation for sleep. For this session, we will relax the mind and body so thoroughly that you can go straight to bed after this so you would have a night of restful sleep. That way, you will wake the next day feeling fully refreshed and energized.

So to begin, lay back into a comfortable position on your bed. You can place your arms and legs however you like so long as you are comfortable. Comfort is very essential to relaxation, after all. You don't have to close your eyes yet.

At first, you don't have to do anything but to let go of your body. Allow it to adjust to the mattress. Feel your spine settling back and relaxing. Rest your head back against a pillow if that is your preference, and just savor the relief of simply lying back after an active day.

We will start off this meditation with a simple breathing exercise. So, go ahead and take a deep breath now to let the body know that it is time to unwind and relax. Again, no need to close your eyes or calm your mind yet. Spend some time just on breathing and letting the body loose and relax.

At this point, your mind may wander and bring up random thoughts. Your eyes may wander as well as you practice this breathing exercise. But right now, you don't have to worry about that. Just focus on breathing and bring in as much air into your body as possible to allow it to relax and unwind.

Take another deep breath in through your nose… And through your mouth, as you exhale.

In… And out…

In… And out…

In… And out…

Perfect.

Now, let's work toward relaxing your eyes. As you breathe in, slowly close your eyes. And as you breathe out, open them again. Continue to do this for a minute, feeling how your eyelids become heavier and heavier at each breath you take.

(Pause 1mn)

Your eyes should feel very heavy at this point, so go ahead and close them. No need to squeeze them shut. Just let them fall naturally. As your vision turns to black, shift your focus to your own breathing. You may also breathe as you normally would.

At this point, it's not about trying too hard to control your breathing, instead, it's letting it occur naturally and just being aware of it. Next, we will perform a quick body scan. As you go through with this, you will realize that certain parts of your body are tense, perhaps a lot more than you imagined.

As you do so, you don't have to do much about those areas of tension. Just notice where they are as we will work toward relaxing the entire body immediately after. So, take a moment now and focus on the top of your head, shifting your focus slowly down the body until you reach the tip of your toes. Notice how each area feels.

(Pause 3mns)

Now, as you inhale, hold your breath in for a few seconds. Feel the air going to your forehead and soothing the tension in that area. Then, breathe out, allowing the air to carry the tension away.

As you inhale, feel your eyelids becoming softer and more relaxed. As you exhale, feel how your eyelids become heavier.

On your next breath in, feel the air going to your cheeks and jaw, loosening and relaxing those areas as you exhale.

Continue to focus on each area of your body and breathe in, allowing the cool air to come in and soothe that area, and let it carry away all the tension as you breathe out.

(Pause 3mns)

Simply allow your body to relax completely into the surface and enjoy the support for your body that allows you to totally relax.

(Pause 1mn)

And as you allow your body to relax, simply take the time to notice how each part of your body feels. Notice how your head and neck feel. Notice how your shoulders and arms let go and relax. Your hands and even your fingers relax.

Simply notice how the sensation of calm and relaxation travels along your body from your scalp down your toes. Notice the tingle all the way down your spine. Notice how your breath allows your back and chest to relax.

Your abdomen and your hips relax into the surface beneath you. As you continue to allow your body to relax. Notice how your thighs and calves relax and let go. Notice how your feet and toes relax and notice the sounds around you now.

(Pause 2mn)

These sounds are all adding to your relaxation. Continue to breathe deeply through your nose and deeply into our belly in and out. Deeper and deeper, more and more calm and happy…

Just let my voice and any of the sounds help you to relax.

And now bring your attention to your mind. Allow your mind to simply let go of any resistant thoughts that you may have. Allow your mind to relax and allow any thoughts to simply pass.

And smile, knowing how grateful you are to take time out to heal your body, mind, and spirit. And as you allow your mind and body to let go, just listen to my soft soothing voice. Bring your awareness back to your breathing as you are now wonderfully and deeply relaxed.

(Pause 1mn)

Your mind is calm, your body is still and totally relaxed. You feel the wonderful sense of deep relaxation.

(Pause 1mn)

Feel your body sinking deeper and deeper into the state of relaxation at every breath that you take.

Now, take a moment and imagine that you are standing in a void, with a giant wooden door in front of you. You walk toward this door. The door has intricate and very detailed carvings and feels cold to the touch. The handle is adorned in gold, but as you touch it, you feel like something is amazing on the other side.

What lies in wait on the other side?

As you push the door open, the light on the other side floods your vision. As your vision adjusts to the light, your heart gladdens at the sight. It is a place that you have always dreamed of seeing.

Take a moment now and the picture that you are standing in this very place. It does not matter where it is. It could be at the top of a tall mountain. It could be at the beach. It could be in the forest. It could be fictitious or real. It does not matter. Let your mind conjure this place into existence.

Feel how it would be like to remain in this place of peace. Feel the warmth or coolness of this place. Feel this place with all your senses.

(Pause 2mns)

Did you know how your mind create this place? This place has always been there. This is a place where you visit unconsciously when you are sleeping. It is just there, a product of your mind. It knows just the right thing to help it relax.

The only problem in the past is that you stumble upon this place irregularly and unconsciously. When you are in this place, you would feel very relaxed and energized the next day. But when you leave, you cannot return to this place. You did not know how.

But now that you are in this place, take a moment to enjoy everything that it has to offer. Let this magical place fill you with relaxation and energy. Allow it to relax your mind, body, and soul.

(Pause 3mns)

As we come to the end of this meditation, take another short moment to appreciate this place. While you had not been able to visit this place consciously in the past, you are here right now. You can take this place, and its relaxing aura, with you to the outside world.

Whenever you feel stressed or tense, you can always come back to this place. All you have to do is to give this place a name and a symbol. The name is so that you can find this place again, and the symbol is the key to unlock this place. So go ahead and think of a name and a symbol that represent this place. Your mind created this place, so let it speak to you.

(Pause 1mn)

Now that you made sure that you can visit this place in the future, talk a walk through this place one more time, toward the big wooden door that you just came through. In the future, when you wish to return to this place, just close your eyes and breathe. Recall the name of this magical place and imagine the symbol that you gave this place to access it. Then, you will be able to enjoy the relaxing aura and rejuvenate your soul.

Now you are standing in front of the big wooden door. Take a final look at this magical place and walk through the door, back into the void.

The door closes behind you with a soft thud. You are standing in the void again, but this time feeling much better than you were before.

Take a deep breath now and prepare to decent back into the outside world. As I count to 5, feel your sensations returning to your body.

1… Slowly coming back to your body…

2… Feel your lungs expand and contract as you breathe…

3… Wiggle your fingers and toes now…

4… Feel the environment around you…

5… And you have returned. Thank you and goodnight.

Deep Sleep Meditation (60mns)

Hello and welcome to this deep sleep meditation. It is intended to relax both the body and mind so that you could get a restful sleep. This is important that you get a dreamless sleep as any dreams that you may have, both good and bad, will affect your emotions when you wake up. Most of the time, it will only make you feel more tired at the start of the day.

With a restful sleep, you will wake up feeling refreshed and energized for the day ahead. So this is what we will be working toward.

To begin, lay down in your bed facing up and place your arms and legs however you like so long as you are comfortable. Comfort is of utmost importance for deep relaxation, and relaxation is necessary for sleep, just as your mind may find it easier if you use memory and imagination for worrying. You can just as easily learn to use them to help you relax. You can sleep without worrying after you have completed this meditation.

First, you need to give your mind a break from your worries. Start with a simple breathing exercise to quieten the mind. You don't even have to close your eyes or focus on your breathing yet. All you have to do now is just remain with my voice and breathe deeply. Let's begin.

In through your nose, take a deep breath from the stomach, letting the air fill your lungs completely.

Hold your breath for a few seconds.

Then, through the mouth, exhale slowly, feeling the air exiting your body.

Do this for a few minutes to allow the body to relax.

(Pause 3mns)

Now that your body is thoroughly relaxed. We can start to relax the eyes. So, continue to breathe as you normally would. But as you inhale, close your eyes gently. As you exhale, open your eyes again. Continue to do this for a while until your eyelids start to become heavy.

(Pause 2mns)

Your eyelids should feel so heavy that you are struggling to keep your eyes open now. When that happens, go ahead and let them fall down naturally. No need to squeeze your eyes shut or anything. Just let your vision turn dark. As it does, shift your focus to your own breathing.

Then, let your mind become quiet. Turn your attention inward as you focus on relaxing your body. Let your muscles relax. Feel this relaxation washing from the top of your head to the tip of your toes.

Let us check in with the body and mind.

Start to scan your entire body and noting any tension in your body as well as noticing where you feel a lightness or ease.

Then, scan your emotional body to notice any feelings or stress as well as emotional lightness, or something you feel good about…

Then, check in with your mind. Notice if today is one of those days full of worrying thoughts. Or if today is a good day and that you feel peaceful and quiet….

Then, focus on your breathing. Notice how it flows in and out of your body. Feel the air as it fills and deflates your lungs. Notice how your chest gently rises and falls at each breath you take.

You may notice that the air does not flow as smoothly. Maybe your breaths are shallow. Maybe you feel constrained. You can start to take deeper breaths. First into the belly.

In…

And out…

Then from the chest…

In…

And out…

Then focus on your upper back as you breathe…

In…

And out…

Now, repeat the breathing cycle again but holding the breath, starting from the belly…

In…

Hold…

And out…

From the chest…

In…

Hold…

And out…

Focusing on your upper back now…

In…

Hold…

And out…

Breathe deep and slow…

As you breathe, imagine the tension in your physical body releasing from your nose. As you breathe, scan through your body again and notice any tense muscles in your body.

Let your breathing soothes those muscles… As if the air you let out takes away the tension in your body. You may notice that your face is tense, or you may notice certain areas of your body are tense that you did not realize before. You can only see them once you are in deep relaxation…

So, breathe…

In…

And out…

Now, imagine what relaxation feels like. It may be warm, heavy. Or light. Tingly. Loose. Relaxation is a calm, pleasant feeling. It feels very comfortable.

Let your muscles relax. Note any areas where your muscles are tense… Let us focus on relaxation from there. As your chest rises and falls gently at each breath, imagine how relaxing every time you breathe out. As your chest lowers as you exhale, you feel even more relaxed.

As you breathe out, imagine all the tension leaves your body, riding on the air you let out of your chest. And you become even more relaxed as you breathe in the cool air. Becoming so deeply relaxed. Notice how relaxed you are.

As you breathe, any remaining tension continues to leave your body. And you become more and more relaxed. You need to rest. Any sleep is helpful, no matter how short it is. As long as you can get some rest, it is worthwhile. Even a short, shallow sleep is great.

Right now, during the night, it is the best time for you to relax, rest. and sleep. Even just relaxing like this can help you feel refreshed. It can restore your mind and body. It is okay if you fall asleep right now. Just relaxing like this is enough.

As you continue to breathe, know that you will feel fully energized when you wake up the next day. You will feel thoroughly rested, refreshed, and alert. You will wake up when you need to. At this very moment, for the time being, just rest.

Relax.

Take all the time you need to sleep, to relax.

Now, let's start to relax the body first. To do this, start to scan your entire body from the top of your head to the tip of your toes, noting any tension in your body.

Let's start with thoroughly relaxing your entire body. As you inhale, feel the air loosening up your throat and feel your neck resting on the pillow. Feel it sink into the ground, fully supported. Try not to hold any parts of your body in any position. Relax and let them fall into their natural resting position.

Next, shift your focus to your shoulders. Let them sink deeper into the mattress. Relax. Let go of all the weight on your chest. Relax your entire arms. Feel them becoming limp. Let your fingers come to rest in their natural curl.

Maintain your deep and slow breathing.

In…

Hold…

And out…

As you continue to breathe, focus on relaxing your chest. Feel the air undoing any tension coils that bind your chest. Release the tension across your ribs, middle back, and lower back. Let your body sink deeper and deeper into the mattress. Notice how it feels as it sinks into it.

Now, relax the abdomen, hips, and buttocks. Loosen up those muscles. Then, focus on relaxing the thighs, knees, and ankles. Let those calves muscles loose.

Let them soften up as you breathe slowly and deeply…

In…

Hold…

And out…

Finally, focus on relaxing the feet. Again, do not hold them still in one place. Let them fall to their natural position. Let your toes fall out to the sides.

Now, take another deep breath, and scan your body as you do so.

In…

Hold…

And out…

Right now, you should feel your muscles become very limp. Feel the tenderness in your muscles that were once plagued with tension and stress. Even if there is still some tension remaining, they will be swept away by your breathing. A little more will be gone with every exhale.

Now, do not worry about where you need to be next or what you need to do.

Right now, allow yourself the time to intentionally relax. You can still take note of any emotional stress, as it will occur during this meditation session. Just like your physical stress, you will exhale it away with your smooth breath.

In…

Hold…

And out…

Let your breathing send out any unwanted stress…

Allow your mind to rest on the sensation of each breath…

In, though the nose…

And out, through the nose…

As you breathe out, take a moment to check your body and mind. Look for any signs of stress. Follow along with me and let us work through the body once again.

Now, let's work through the body once more.

Again, release the jaws and the muscles of your face.

Breathe in slowly, holding it at the top, and let it out smoothly.

Focus on relaxing your entire body once more…

Relaxing the shoulders,

Relaxing the abdomen,

The hips, and the legs.

Feel your body completely supported by the cushion and the ground beneath you…

Focus on your breathing now, and notice where it flows into your body and where it doesn't.

Feel the air going through your belly, chest, and upper back before you exhale…

Breathe in…

Hold…

And out…

Inhale into the belly, then the chest…

Imagine the air going throughout your entire body, bringing healing energy to every fiber of your being. Feel your entire body becoming soft, tender, and very relaxed. As you breathe, feel the air going to every nook and cranny of your body.

Feel the air going to your arms, legs, fingertips, toes, ribs, hips, neck, head, and ears. Feel your body being nourished as you breathe. Feel it being nourished with energy and relaxation.

At each breath, you take in nourishment your body needs, and let out any stress and tension in your body and mind…

Continue to breathe as you start to clear your mind from any mental chatter, allowing it to be fully focused on sensing the entire body.

Imagine you inhaling clarity, a sense of well-being, and calm, and let them manifest in your body as you hold your breath at the top, and then release stress…

At each breath you take in, you fortify, strengthen, and refresh the body. At each exhale, you let go of all that no longer serves you…

Breathe slowly and deeply…

In…

Hold…

And out…

Now, let us work toward relaxing the mind and give it a rest from the chaos in this world. Give yourself a mental vacation by taking your mind to that place of happiness. Whenever worrying thoughts intrude your peace of mind, as they will, recall this serene feeling you have in your body at this very moment.

Whenever your peace of mind is intruded by worldly worries, tell yourself to breathe… The rise and fall of your chest will soothe you. Let yourself relax.

Then, imagine that worry is a deep and dark place. And peace you crave for is the light. Worry tells you a simple message: Stay awake because of me. It is full of darkness and tension just like the one you felt in your muscles, even if you are lying in bed. This is what worry does to your mind. It forces you to remain awake until the sun rises once more.

If you are afraid to go to bed because darkness brings worries to the surface, embrace words about light and peace in your mind and relaxation in your body with steady and calm breathing.

Picture your peace of mind as a place of beautiful light, a place of comfort. It will call to you. They will call upon you to go to where you will be cozy, relaxed, and energized. Maybe you are picturing a nice warm bed that you are currently sleeping on. But this place is more than that. This place of peace will take away all your worries and allow your exhausted mind to be free from all stress in life. It is a place of beautiful tranquility.

Imagine this peaceful place. It could be one beyond your wildest dreams, a magnificent waterfall, a vast field of vibrant flowers, a mountaintop that pierces the clouds, a golden beach, or a thick and peaceful forest… It could be a place you have been to… Use the power of your imagination to access that place of peace.

Bring peaceful words or music to yourself. If you wake up and cannot get back to sleep, or if worries take you away from the peaceful place, say to yourself,

"I can do something about this by putting peaceful words in my mind and access the place of peace once more… Or calming music… Until I can get to that place again. Right now, I am in my bed, surrounded by soft, fluffy pillows. I am not in danger. Nothing can harm me. I am at peace. I can picture happy images with my imagination. I can recall peaceful words I have read or heard today to calm me down. I can listen to new peaceful, sleepy words that can lead me to dreamy, wonderful places."

Let both relaxation and sleep come to you naturally. Let the subconscious mind take control. Let my soft and gentle words carry you into a very relaxing and restful sleep. Let the words work their magic. Imagine the words you whisper to yourself coming to life and take you to that peaceful place. Better yet, imagine them carrying you away into sleep on a cloud, or the words themselves are soft cozy beds.

Know those worrying thoughts tell your brain to stay awake as they cause tight sensations in your body and thoughts that repeat again and again in your mind. Imagine them being swept away by your breath as you breathe out, and whatever is left is erased by the kind words you whisper to yourself.

With all your worries gone, allow yourself to drift deeper and deeper into the state of peace, tranquility, and relaxation. Repeat to yourself:

"I cannot relax if I force myself to relax…"

"Instead, I let relaxing words guide me… They can cause my mind and body to relax and deliver me to my peaceful place…"

"My body knows how to breathe… It can do this naturally."

"If I wake up and cannot fall asleep, I can just relax… and let the kind words bring me back to that peaceful place…"

"When I am aware that I've woken up, this is a cue to begin a relaxing routine… To attain mental tranquility…"

"It is okay to wake briefly during the night…"

"When I am aware that I cannot sleep, I tell myself to whisper relaxing words to myself…"

"My goal is to relax… Not sleep…"

"Rest and relaxation help my body rejuvenate."

Excellent.

Take your time to enjoy this unhurried moment. Allow yourself to immerse in meditation and give your body and mind full attention. Notice any tense areas in your body or mind and breathe away to relax them.

As you come to the end of this meditation session, take another deep breath and smile as you have given yourself time and attention. Continue maintaining this deep breathing until you fall asleep…

Thank you and goodnight.

Sleep talkdown 1 (10mns)

Hello and welcome to this sleep talkdown meditation. To begin, get into a comfortable position on your bed. That way, we can send you right off to sleep after this meditation session concludes.

It does not matter how you lie or sit down, so long as you are comfortable. Comfort is essential to achieve deep relaxation, after all. Right now, you do not need to close your eyes yet. Just take 5 deep breaths to signal to the body that it is time to unwind, relax, and sleep.

Breathe in through your nose… Letting the air fill your lungs completely… Then breathe out…

Very good. Now, do that again.

In… And out…

In… And out…

In… And out…

In… And out…

Now, you may close your eyes and bring your focus to your breathing. Again, breathe in deep, holding your breath for a few seconds before you exhale. Allow your breath to carry away any physical and emotional burden in your body and mind.

Continue to breathe deeply and slowly, allowing your body to relax. Allow your breath to hold your focus in the present moment.

(Pause 2mns)

You may now breathe as you normally would. As you continue to breathe, you may notice that your mind starts to bring up random thoughts that may stress you. If this happens, gently guide your focus back to your breathing. No point in beating yourself up for it.

As you continue to breathe, let us give color to the air that you bring into your body. Let's say that it has a light and bright blue color to it. Feel its healing aura as you breathe in, feeling the color going to all parts of your body and soothing any pain that you may have.

As you breathe out, imagine that the air becomes dark orange as it brings with it the stress and tension in your body.

Take a long, slow deep breath in through your nose and now move the breath all the way down into your abdomen, filling you up with light and making space. Relax and let your body let go, let go of everything as you breathe out. Let go of anything that is of no use to you.

Continue breathing to allow your body to relax…

(Pause 2mns)

Stay with your breath. When you find your mind wandering, stay with the physical sensations of your body so that your mind can continue to clear the clutter of the overthinking tendency.

In this very moment, you are in complete control. Both the mind and body know that now is the time to relax. In this very moment, you just need to focus on your breathing and allow your body to sink deeper into the state of relaxation.

Continue to breathe and relax. Remain with your breath. Allow it to soothe your body, mind, and soul. You can always bring this relaxation with you no matter where you are. You can use this relaxation to calm the mind after a long day and attain a night of restful sleep. That way, you will wake up the next day feeling energized.

In just a moment, I will count to 10. You will begin to bring your awareness back to the present moment, feeling relaxed and ready to go to sleep.

1… You are slowly beginning to come out of the state of comfort.

2… You are feeling totally relaxed and calm.

3…

4… Your mind is clear and calm.

5…

6… Your thoughts are positive.

7….

8… You begin to bring some gentle movements to your body.

9…

10… Thank you and goodnight.

Sleep talkdown 2 (10mns)

Hello and welcome to this sleep talkdown meditation. At the end of this meditation session, you will achieve a deep state of relaxation and be able to get a deep and restful sleep. That way, you will wake up the next day feeling fully energized and ready for the day ahead.

To begin, get into a comfortable position. It does not matter if you are sitting or lying down on your bed. So long as you are comfortable, you can remain wherever you are. After all, comfort is very important or relaxation.

At this point, you don't even have to close your eyes yet. Just breathe deeply from your stomach, letting and feeling the air fill your lungs completely before breathing out again. Do this a couple of times to let your body and mind know that it is time to unwind and relax.

(Pause 1mn)

Your mind and eyes may wander at this point. This is quite alright. Allow them to wander as they please for now. We will focus on calming the mind later.

Now, as you breathe in, close your eyes. As you exhale, open your eyes again. Do this a couple of times and feel your eyelids becoming heavier and heavier as you continue to breathe.

(Pause 1mn)

At this point, your eyelids should be very heavy. Allow them to fall down naturally without forcing your eyes shut. Turn your attention to your breath.

Take another deep breath, this time feeling how the air goes into your body. As you breathe out, feel the air exiting your body.

Take another deep breath, holding it in at the top, and then breathe out. Continue to breathe this way for a couple of minutes.

(Pause 2mns)

You may breathe at your natural rhythm. As you continue to breathe, you may notice that your mind starts to wander again. No need to beat yourself up for it. Simply and gently guide your focus back to your breathing.

Now, picture yourself laying in a large field of grass, looking up at the night sky full of flickering stars. The night is calm and the sky is clear. You can see the stars flickering as you breathe in and out. It is as if the entire universe is in sync with your mind and soul.

As you lay there, staring at the night sky, feel a gentle breeze brushing up against you as you breathe. Feel this cool breeze seeping into your body and soothing the aches and tensions in your body.

You feel your body is entirely supported by the surface beneath you. Every time you breathe, feel your body sinking deeper into the surface and into relaxation. As you breathe, surrender yourself to the universe, knowing full well that it will take care of you.

As you sink deeper and deeper into the state of relaxation, remind yourself of how hard you have been working for the past few days. Maybe you are going through a rough time. Maybe you are burnt out after all that work. No matter what you are going through right now, now is not the time to worry about such things.

Now is the time for relaxation. Now is the time to rejuvenate. Now is the time to take a break from the chaos of this world and just focus on relaxation, peace, and tranquility.

You know that you can only push your body and mind so far before you start to tire. Your body and mind need to take a break once in a while. You know this and you chose to give the body and mind the time and space they need to recover.

You chose to take care of yourself first. It is not selfish to put your needs above others sometimes. Only when you are functioning at full capacity can you help others effectively. You chose to care for your body and mind, and this is the best gift you can give yourself.

Take a moment now to smile and thank yourself for forgiving yourself this opportunity to rejuvenate. Thank yourself because you chose to take care of yourself. You might have neglected yourself in the past. Now is the perfect moment to give yourself all the love and care that you deserve.

As we come to the conclusion of this meditation session, I will count to 5. As I do so, slowly bring your consciousness back into your body.

1… Slowly bringing your consciousness back…

2… Bringing along the relaxation…

3… Bringing along the peace and tranquility

4… Coming back now…

5… Thank you and goodnight.

Deep Relaxation Guided Meditation (30mns)

Hello and welcome to this deep relaxation guided meditation. In this session, we will work toward giving your body that much-needed break from the chaos of this world, to free you from tension and stress, and give you a sense of physical and mental calmness.

To begin, simply get into a comfortable position. You can lie down or sit straight up, whatever makes you feel the most comfortable. Comfort is very important to relaxation, after all.

But before you close your eyes, let's go through a simple breathing exercise first. This is to tell the body that it is time to unwind and relax.

First, take a deep breath in. Let the air fills your lungs. Then breathe out, emptying your lungs.

Take another deep breath through your nose. Let the air out through your mouth.

Breathe in…

And out…

In…

Out…

Keep this slow and steady breathing, completely filling and emptying your lungs at each breath.

Your deep breathing relaxes and calms you. It allows your body to relax, to get enough oxygen, and to feel calm. Please breathe like this for a couple of minutes.

(Pause 2mns)

Now, your body is ready for relaxation. As you breathe in, close your eyes. As you breathe out, open your eyes again. Continue to do this for another minute until your eyelids become heavy.

(Pause 1mn)

Your eyelids should feel very heavy right now. You can go ahead and close your eyes, letting the weight pulling your eyelids downward. As your vision goes dark, shift your focus to your own breathing.

Focus on your breathing. Remain in this position. There is nothing you need to do right now and nowhere you need to be. You just need to be here, relax, and enjoy this time for yourself.

Enjoy this relaxation meditation. You have been through a lot. You deserve and need this time for yourself to function at your best. This relaxation time will help you to be calm and healthy. This session is your productive, health time. You are doing yourself a favor by taking care of your mental health with this sleep anxiety relaxation meditation.

As you maintain your deep and steady breathing, turn your attention to your body. Notice how it feels physically. Do not do anything about it. Just be aware of the sensations in your body.

Take a moment now and scan your body, from the top of your head. Notice how your forehead feels. Maybe it is tense in sheer concentration. Loosen up and relax… Loosen up the jaw. Allow your tongue to loosen up and settle down in your mouth.

If your shoulders are tense, loosen them up as well. Continue to observe and loosen up each area as you go, breathing in deeply to relax those places if you need to. Scan your entire body, from the top of your head and move downward slowly. Notice each area as you focus your attention on it. Observe how your body feels.

Keep scanning your body. Gradually focus your attention on lower and lower parts of your body. How does your upper body feel? Note any areas of tension.

As you move to the center of your body, around the level of your stomach, note how this part of your body is feeling. Keep observing your physical state. Continue to scan your body as you shift your focus lower and lower.

Keep doing this to the level of your hips. Keep observing and shifting your attention down. How do you feel at this part of your body? Notice tensions in this part without trying to change anything. Once again, move your focus downward.

At the level of your knees, again, notice how this area feels. Note any tension. Continue to scan your body now… Going to the very tip of your toes.

Now, take another moment to scan your entire body. Note how your body feels as a whole. Where do you feel the tensest?

Starting with the tensest area, focus hard on that one area. Feel how your muscles feel in that area. Take a deep breath and feel the muscles in those areas loosening up and letting go of their tension. Imagine them relaxing, releasing the tension bit by bit until the area relax.

Feel the tension softening in your body. Feel the muscles loosening up, bit by bit. Feel them stretching, warming, and relaxing, as if they are melting.

Note where your body the most relaxed. How does it feel? Imagine this sensation to be warm, tingly, moving, growing, and spreading to other parts of your body. Think of it as an aura that flows slowly through your body.

Feel your body becoming more and more relaxed as the aura spreads throughout your body as you continue this meditation.

Now, imagine that the air you breathe in is the energy you need to relax. Imagine that the air you breathe in is relaxation, and the air you exhale is the stress and tension in your body. Imagine that the breathing you have been doing is an efficient relaxation system.

Feel this relaxation as you take each and every breath. Expel the tension in your body as you exhale through your mouth. Continue to take in relaxation through the nose and push out tension through your mouth. Continue doing this as you let your body relax.

Feel the relaxed area growing bigger as you breathe in, and the tension areas getting smaller as you breathe out.

Breathe in…

And breathe out…

Every breath that you take adds more and more into the relaxation. As you exhale, you push away the tension. Keep your breathing slow and steady. Feel how your body starts to become more and more relaxed at every breath you take.

Soon, you will realize that the areas of tension become very small at each breath you take. Eventually, the last bit of tension will be washed away with your breathing. You now feel calm, relaxed. Your system is clean… Breathing in relaxation and breathing out relaxation.

Take a deep breath in… and relax…

Now, breathe out… Relax…

Keep your breathing slow and steady. Maintain your pace and feel your body relaxing more and more deeply with each breath you take. As you continue this meditation, scan through your body again. Notice how your body feels now. Start from the top of your head… and move down… to the tips of your toes…

(Pause 1mn)

Now, imagine that your body is like a hard, solid piece of chocolate. But the warmth radiating from your core is your heart, the center of emotion. Imagine this familiar warmth soften the rigid body of yours.

Soon, your hands and feet will feel soft as if they are melting into liquid. As the warmth spreads throughout your body, radiating from your heart to your arms, legs, and head, feel them melting softly. This is a pleasant and very relaxing feeling.

Feel this warm slowly softening up the core of your body. Take a deep breath now and relax as this warmth relaxes and melts your body. Feel this warmth spreading to your hands and feet.

Now, imagine that your body is very soft just like melted chocolate that is soft and smooth. You do not need anything now. Just rest and enjoy this relaxing sensation.

(Pause 2mns)

Now, focus on your thoughts. Notice your calm thoughts as you are enjoying this relaxation.

You can attain complete calm and relaxation just by focusing on a single word. Meditate now and focus on the word "relax" by mentally saying it each time you breathe in and out.

Breathe in, "relax"

Breathe out, "relax"

Continue your slow and steady breathing, saying "relax" in your mind each time you breathe in and again when you breathe out. Continue doing this for a couple of minutes.

(Pause 2mns)

It is okay if your thoughts start to wander, as they will. Gently guide your focus back on the word "relax". Keep repeating this word as you continue your meditation.

(Pause 2mns)

Focus… Relax…

Keep repeating this word…

Notice how your body and mind are completely relaxed and calm. Notice how you are slowly drifting into a state of relaxation and sleepiness. You can let your mind drift. Now is the time to let your mind wander. You do not need to focus on anything at all.

Just… Rest… Relax… And enjoy this pleasant state you are in.

(Pause 1mn)

Keep relaxing for a while longer…

Enjoy this pleasant, calm feeling…

Enjoy this time you have earned for yourself…

You deserve the best…

This feeling of calm and confidence will be there by your side as you about your daily life, even when you encounter stress… You may even be able to bring this relaxed feeling with you even when you encounter stressful situations…

Imagine the confidence and composure you will display as you face stress while still feeling calm.

Take a deep breath in…

Relaxation breathing…

And breathe out… Emptying your longs…

Keep breathing calmly and smoothly… Maintain this breathing cycle… Taking in relaxation and pushing out the tension that accumulates throughout the day… Imagine how every breath you take helps you become resilient against the harsh reality of life… That you are now able to cope with the stresses that come your way…

(Pause 1mn)

As we come to the conclusion of this meditation session, take a moment to open your eyes and smile… Stretch if you must… Rub your hands together and move your feet gently… You are very relaxed. Thank you and have a nice day.

Stress Relieving Morning Meditation (20mns)

Hello and welcome to this stress-relieving morning meditation. To begin, get into a comfortable position. You can either remain in your bed or sit in your living room, whatever you are comfortable with. Comfort is very important for a productive meditation session, after all.

Before we dive deep into this meditation, I would like you to start with a simple breathing exercise. Without closing your eyes or focus on anything, in particular, take a very deep breath from your stomach. Follow the flow of the air as it goes into your body through your nostrils.

Continue to do this for a minute.

(1mns)

Perfect. Now, allow your eyes to close and your focus to settle on your own breathing. As you breathe, you may have thoughts going through your mind. That's okay. Notice them from afar as if you are an observer.

Now, begin to deepen each breath

in…

and out…

As you continue to breathe, shift your focus to the silence, the pause, between your inhale and exhale. Hold your breath at the top for a few seconds and savor that moment of perfect stillness. Allow the stillness to last a little longer, pausing, holding the breath momentarily between the inhale and the exhale.

Breathe in this way for a few more cycles and feel the tension melt away from your body to be gone forever.

(Pause 1mn)

Give yourself permission to be fully supported by your surroundings and be open to the possibility of what comes with a state of comfort.

Allow your mind to quiet and the noises and responsibilities of the world around you to turn off. Soon, we will work on relaxing the body. We will do so by using the power of your focus and your breathing to target areas of tension and soothe them through breathing alone.

So, go ahead now and bring your awareness to your body. Look for any signs of tension, starting from the top of your head to the tips of your toes.

(Pause 1mn)

When you notice any tense areas, focus on your breathing to soothe that area. Go over your body a few more times, focus on every nook and cranny of your body, especially your jaw.

(Pause 2mns)

What other sensations do you notice at this moment?

The simple process of noticing your breath, your physical body, and your surroundings is such a powerful tool for relaxation and stress relief.

Let go of any remaining tension. your body feels to be completely relaxed, safe, and supported.

Follow the sound of my voice on this journey of relaxation, take notice of any thoughts that come into your mind. All you have to do now is to notice their existence. Remain where you are and watch as they come and go in flashes, just like the shooting start in the vastness of your mind.

Now, using your imaginative mind, picture a white cloud, soft and fluffy, rising from the ground. This cloud will be your personal steed. This could carry you to relaxation, away from the worldly worries.

This cloud is special and it is just for you when you lay down on this cloud.

It fits you perfectly. It supports you entirely so you can let go of any need for holding on. Take a journey on this cloud as it will drift you off to your most favorite peaceful place. Using the power of your imaginative mind, conjure this place in vivid detail. It can be any place that you are happy and that place is perfect for you.

You are at peace with yourself. You are very relaxed and calm. You could feel that it is not too hot or too cold for you. In fact, the temperature is just right for you. You feel at ease. So, take a moment now and see yourself in this very tranquil place. Take in all the surroundings with your senses.

This is your safe haven. This is where you can feel relaxed. This is where you can let go completely. This is your personal space. Here, nothing bad can happen to you.

(Pause 2mns)

You are safe and supported. You are completely in control.

You are completely relaxed in this happy place. In just a moment I'm going to count down from 10 to 1 and as I do, you can allow yourself to relax completely on the soft cloud. Take a deep breath now to feel the relaxation and comfort in this very special place just for you. Allow yourself to relax more and more.

I will start to count now…

10… Let yourself go completely.

9…

8… You are fully relaxed…

7… Relax…

6… You are in full control…

5…

4… Your relaxation continues to double with each number

3…

2… Deeper into comfort

And 1… all the way into a deep relaxation…

Focus on breathing deeply, allowing yourself to relax and focus on calming the body…

(Pause 3mns)

Now, let go of any negative thoughts that do not serve you. Let go of any past negativities and replace them with positive thoughts and gratitude.

In just a moment, I will count to 5.

When I get to 5, you will awaken from the state of relaxation to the present moment, feeling relaxed yet energizing, confident when you awake you will still feel this way.

1… You are beginning to come out of the state of comfort.

2… You are feeling relaxed… Begin to bring some gentle movements to your body

3… your mind is clear and confident, feeling wonderful emotionally calm and at peace…

4… You feel the strength of your confidence and you believe in yourself

5… Open your eyes you are fully awake and energized.

Post Work Stress Relieving Meditation (20mns)

Hello and welcome to this post-work stress relieving meditation. In this session, you shall use the power of your imagination to comfort and calm your mind after a long day of work.

At the end of the day, it is important to become thoroughly relaxed so you can enjoy your time at home. It is even more important that you get a full, restful sleep so you have the energy to tackle tomorrow's tasks.

First, make yourself comfortable on your bed and take a few, slow, and deep breaths and notice that as you exhale, you feel yourself becoming more relaxed.

You can continue to relax as you listen and breathe. Each time you exhale, you can feel yourself becoming more and more relaxed.

More and more relaxed…

Soon, you will experience relaxation and you are probably wondering what that experience will be like.

Rest assured that no matter how deeply relaxed you become, you will remain in complete control. You will stay in control even when you are very deeply immersed in the experience of relaxation.

As you breathe, you can feel yourself becoming more and more relaxed, but no matter how relaxed you become, focus on listening as we go along on this guided meditation session.

At any point during this meditation session, you can readjust your position so long as you feel comfortable. Do not let discomfort get in the way of your experience of relaxation.

Now, imagine a spreading sense of calm and peace spreading throughout your body. Let go of all of your cares and concerns. Let them drift away like clouds in the wind, dissipating more and more.

Let your entire body relax as you pay attention to each part of your body, starting from the head and work your way toward the tip of your toes. Feel each and every part of your body loosening up and going limb. Feel every single muscle in your body relaxing as you breathe.

Now that your body is entirely at ease, you can start to imagine being somewhere peaceful and relaxing. Perhaps you can picture yourself sunbathing on a quiet beach on a warm sunny day with a beautiful blue sky. But you can imagine being anywhere you like, even in fictional locations. So long as you can feel relaxed and at ease, it is perfect.

That place should be a safe haven for you, somewhere you want to be, or where you can be yourself. You can imagine yourself being there with your mind's eye, and since all the things your body would sense.

Now, as you are in your perfect place, count to ten. As I count, feel yourself drifting more and more into relaxation.

1…

2…

3…

4…

5… Halfway there…

6…

7…

8…

9… Almost there…

10…

You are now very deeply relaxed, completely at one with yourself, completely engrossed. Now, focus solely on your special place. Just be there now and know that you are at peace. Calm and relaxed.

There is no tension, no anxiety. Concentrate on this feeling and know that you can take it with you throughout your day tomorrow. No stress or anxiety shall intrude on your mental tranquility. Whenever you are stressed, you can turn to your special place and breathe to allow your body to be calm once more.

Finally, take another deep breath and smile. You may now enjoy the rest of the day and be assured that you get a restful sleep.

Anxiety Meditation (15mns)

Hello and welcome to this anxiety reduction meditation. To begin, simply get into a comfortable position. You can sit or lie down, whichever is comfortable for you. Comfort is important for relaxation, after all.

Once you are nicely settled in, take a deep breath. Feel the air flowing into your nose, filling up your lungs. As you exhale, feel the air flowing out of your body, taking with it the stress you had been holding in.

Perfect. Now, breathe in again, and out.

In… And out…

In… And out…

Excellent. Your mind may wander as you continue to breathe. Your mind may bring up something that makes you feel anxious. Whenever that happens, gently push those thoughts aside and say, "I'll handle that later."

Continue to breathe in deeply through your nose, letting the air fill up your lungs completely. Then, breathe out slowly through your mouth, feeling the air flowing through your body.

Spend some time to stay with your breathing, focusing on any of its elements to keep you anchored at the moment. Push aside any worrying thoughts for now.

This is the time you make for yourself to just relax. This is the time you need to unwind and rejuvenate. This is the time to take a break from a stressful life. At this very moment, all you have to do is relax and not think about anything else.

There is a time and place for worrying but now is not the time. Right now, you are giving yourself the space you need to clear your head. You are allowing your soul to rejuvenate. This is a wonderful gift you can give yourself.

(Pause 2mns)

Take a moment now to thank yourself for this opportunity to relax. You should perhaps take care of yourself more. You have been working so hard for the last several days. Maybe you are just burnt out. Maybe you are worrying too much. Maybe it's just a sign that you have reached your limit and you need to take a break.

Whatever the case may be, tell yourself that worrying will not solve any problems. If anything it just makes things a lot worse for you. It could hinder your performance. It could drain your energy. It could take away your motivation and creativity.

Anxiety is a very scary monster because it is just that, scary. Its power rests with its ability to scare you into inaction. The best way to chase away that monster is through recognition and action.

Collecting your thoughts and recognizing this problem is the first step in easing your anxiety. Meditation is the best cure for anxiety because it allows you to see the real world through an objective perspective. You are simply taking a step back from all that chaos, refusing to get caught up.

Meditation takes your mind off the problem, allowing you to take a step back and form a more objective view on things. It calms the mind and body, but it might also open up a new path that will solve all your problems.

Now, as we come to the conclusion of this meditation session, slowly bring your consciousness back. Bring your soul back into your body and take another deep breath. Slowly open your eyes and stretch your limbs. Smile, because you deserve happiness. Things will get better.

Thank you and take care.

Meditation for Reducing Anxiety (30mns)

Hello and welcome to this meditation for reducing anxiety. To begin, get into a comfortable position, either sitting upright or laying down. Before we dive into this meditation, I want you to loosen up the body a bit with a simple breathing exercise.

Through your nose, take a deep breath in and fill your stomach, hold it for a few seconds, and then let go. Continue to do this for a short while to signal your body to relax.

(Pause 1mn)

Now that your body is calmer, you can close your eyes right now. Now, I want you to breathe from the stomach again, but without holding it in.

Just breathe in… and out…

In… and out…

In… and out…

Continue to do this for another short while to allow your body to sink deeper into the state of relaxation.

(Pause 1mn)

Now, take a moment and check in with your body. How does it feel? Notice how hot or cold it is. Maybe you are heaving a slight headache. Maybe you feel very warm. Maybe some part of you is aching or itchy.

(Pause 1mn)

Next, take a moment to access your state of mind. Some of us have a very calm mind, hardly thinking random thoughts. Others, which often apply to most of us, have a very active and random mind, like a monkey. It spastically wanders from one thought to another quickly.

Maybe it's one of those days when your mind is unusually cluttered. Maybe you usually have a very clear head, but today feels particularly cloudy. Take a moment to access the state of mind.

(Pause 1mn)

Next, study your emotions. What are you feeling right now? Maybe you don't feel so good. If so, that is fine. We tend to feel down in the dump sometimes. There is no need to do anything right now but relax. Your emotions are very real, but you just have to acknowledge them for now.

You will feel all sorts of emotions, both good or bad. Whatever you do, resist the urge to move toward indulging in the thoughts and feelings that are pleasurable and experience or move away from uncomfortable emotions or painful emotions. Just notice that these feelings exist, both good and bad, and welcome all of them with kindness.

(Pause 1mn)

Now that you have taken the time to come into contact with your mind and body, it is time to dive deeper into relaxation, away from worry, anxiety, stress, and negativity. Return your focus to your breathing. Use it to anchor yourself to the present moment.

Take a deep breath now from your stomach. Feel the cool air entering your body, the air that your body needs to refresh and relax. As you exhale, imagine the air sweeping and carrying away all the stress in your body. Continue to breathe deeply and slowly, counting up to 3 each time.

(Pause 3mns)

Right now, you should feel that your body is slowly loosening up again. You should start to feel a bit drowsy. Your breath brings the air into your body, the air it needs to cleanse itself from the stress you experience throughout the day.

You should feel more and more comfortable now as you continue to breathe deeply and slowly. Now, continue counting and breathing just as before…

(Pause for 2mns)

Note any areas that are still uncomfortable or tense. There may be some thoughts still lingering in your mind as well. Do not try to suppress them. Let them float about in your head, but take note and observe them. The same applies to your body.

From there, focus on the tense muscles or stressful thoughts and start to use the power of your breathing to sweep it away. Imagine you breathing in relaxation and life force, and breathing out stress. Continue to breathe and count as you go.

(Pause for 2mns)

Relax and let the wave of peacefulness and tranquility wash over you. Your head may start to feel heavy. Your body may start to feel limp but heavy as well. Feel every fiber of your muscle relaxing and your body loosening up.

Just continue to keep a gentle and steady breath.

We will count down once again and this time begins to just imagine a bright healing light in front of you. Engulfing you and surrounding you and with each breath, just think of that healing light.

5... See it clearly feel it around you

4... 3... Healing light so vivid...

2... Healing light healing every nerve in your body.

And 1...

Now, shift your focus to the top of your head. As you take another calming and relaxing breath, allow a sensation of relaxing energy to flow down your head, down your head and through your neck, and your

Enjoy the pleasant sensation behind your eyes.

Allow a soothing weight to push down on them as your head gains that feeling of heaviness. Feel that tingling waves move slowly down your arms through your elbows and wrists and out the very tips of your fingers.

Continue to breathe slowly and calmly. Feel the air flowing through your body, in and out. Whenever it comes, feel how relaxing and soothing it is. Whenever it goes out, feel how the air takes away all the stress from your body. Feel the cool air soothing your body, from the top of your head all the way to the tips of your toes. Feel that calming energy coursing through your body.

On these next breaths, just pretend that you're standing elsewhere in the room, watching your own body within the space, and see yourself and visualize it. Imagine that you see a warm glowing light around you now on the next several breaths.

(Pause 2mn)

You might feel that heavy but comforting pressure coming down on your body. Enjoy this sensation, one that feels like you are sleeping under a weighted blanket. Continue to focus on your breath and feel this heaviness anchoring your body to the present moment and instilling within you deep and powerful relaxation.

You will feel that the heavy pressure of weight comes down on you more and more. Enjoy this feeling, this heavy feeling as you take a breath in. Continue to bring focus to your breath. Feel that heaviness pulling you downward into the floor.

Your muscles just relax and give into it…

All down, down, down…

And as you reach the fullness of this weight, take just one minute to soak in this heavy feeling.

Concentrate on that warm glow and relax for one minute…

(Pause 1mn)

What your mind creates is not you. This depression is only a feeling. It's not you. It has you in its grasp. Your suffering is real but hopelessness is not real. The pain that you're running from and is real but the prison bars that you feel trapped behind are not real.

You can overcome this nightmare. You can wake up and find your way out of this dark pit, from this lonely isolated place that you find yourself in. You can and will wait and hang on to hope because it is there for the taking.

It is not lost.

You can escape and you will.

Keep imagining yourself in this warm glow but imagine it change in hue.

It's a vibrant red around you and then slowly becomes a bright blue a bright, glowing blue and the energy begins flowing through you. Notice every nerve, every limb, every part of your body is one within this warm blue glow of light, flowing through you.

Now as I count, you will feel this weight slowly and gently begin to lift…

5… You may suddenly see and visualize the vastness and openness of the sky before you as your body feels light as feathers…

4… You throw off the heavy anvils holding you down to a surface below you…

3… You see yourself no longer bound by gravity or this room

2… Feeling so light and free… Feeling light, free, fearless, and alive…

1… Allow yourself two more minutes. Just two more minutes to float in this open world within your mind.

(Pause 2mns)

Allow yourself to search for these answers that you so desperately know are within…

You give yourself just two minutes of healing.

Take your time to heal but believe in your healing ability.

Believe in your meaning and purpose.

You are still you. You are still alive. You are here you are okay. You are okay. As we come to the end of the meditation, I want you to smile and be happy about the fact that you gave yourself this opportunity to treat your mind and body with the care they need. Smile and be happy as you open your eyes, feeling refreshed, and confident.

Hey! We hope you are enjoying these Guided Meditations/ Bedtime Stories/ Hypnosis, and hope they are helping you as much as humanly possible. We poured our heart and soul into the creation of these, with the sole intention in helping each and every listener such as yourself.

We really appreciate you supporting our mission by purchasing this book, and we don't want to keep you too long, so you can get on with the book of course.

We just wanted to ask you if you could please go over to Audible (once you have finished your session) and leave us a review, as this is the most helpful thing you can do for us as a customer. A review means so much to us, and tells us what parts you enjoyed most, as well as what you would like to see from us in the future.

It also helps us increase the awareness of our work, and be seen by more people, meaning we can help more people, which is exactly our mission, so it really would mean the world if you could do that!

Anyways, now it's time to resume the book, have an amazing day, and enjoy!

Meditation for Managing Panic Attacks (30mns)

Hello and welcome to this meditation for managing panic attacks. In this session, we will work toward relaxing both the mind and body. In the end, you will feel very calm and relaxed.

To begin, I would like you to rest yourself in a comfortable position. You can either sit upright or lie down, whatever works for you. Your arms and legs can be placed anywhere. Comfort is a priority because I want you to be as comfortable as you can be in this meditation. You will be here for quite some time, after all.

Before you close your eyes and dive deep into this meditation session, let us kick off this meditation with a simple breathing exercise to slow the mind and body down a bit.

To do so, just lie or sit there for a while and just breathe. Most of the time, anxiety will go away when you control your breathing, so do that now. Breathe as you normally would before we dive into this meditation.

(Pause 2mns)

Now that both the mind and body is more relaxed, you can start to close your eyes now. Take a deep breath slowly from your nose, letting the air filling your lungs, holding it at the top before letting go through your mouth.

Breathe in… Hold… And out…

In… Hold… And out…

In… Hold… And out…

Very good. Now, continue to do this for another short while.

(Pause 2mns)

Now, loosen up and allow your body to sink a bit deeper into a restful state. You might already be feeling yourself relaxing a little more already just by telling yourself and acknowledging those words.

Feel your body sinking deeper into whatever it is that supports your body. Allow all the muscles in your body to relax.

Now, let us work on relaxing the body as it has a direct influence over the mind. First, allow yourself to check in with your physical sensations. All you have to do is notice how your body feels, particularly where you feel tense. Just take a calm note of whatever that you may experience at this very moment.

Allow all changes to also occur, noticing that as the body does rest and relax, sensations come and go, and continue to change and develop becoming different from moment to moment.

At this point, your mind may start to wander and bring up some worrying thoughts. This is quite alright. At this very moment, your mind may bring up the negative things about a recent or upcoming event that causes your panic.

You do not need to suppress your feelings. All feelings are true, so accept them. They are some of the ways your subconscious mind communicates with your conscious mind. It simply means that you are out of your comfort zone, not in the danger zone.

It is natural for the mind to wander from time to time. Just remain relaxed and calm and notice every passing thought. Remain with each and every thought for a while, but move on by shifting your focus back to your breathing before you get caught up with your thoughts.

Interact with your own thoughts as if you are talking to yourself where one part of you wishes to speak and another part wishes to listen. Listen to your own thoughts and you might perhaps find the root of your misery.

Speaking and listening within yourself in this way, you may find there are certain images. There pictures or glimpses of flashing details which the thinking mind may wish to replay. Think of it like the Story features on Facebook or Instagram.

Your mind is displaying snippets of important moments in your life in short but vivid details, just like scenes from your own personal films, or photographs, or snapshots from your past or from your most immediate and recent day. Simply acknowledge these imageries as they come and go.

For now, let your mind wander as it pleases. Let it direct your focus toward anything and everything, giving it every permission to go there for a moment and then guide it back to your breathing.

(Pause 2mns)

You might think that letting your mind wander is counterintuitive. But suppressing your thoughts might not be the best option, not until done in the right condition. In this case, you want to acknowledge and validate your own emotions before you calm your mind down.

You can only do that when you let your mind wander a bit. It's very important to let the thinking mind know that it does have an important purpose to you and the thinking self can be acknowledged.

You can listen to your own mind to really understand the way you think. The more you do this, the easier it is to understand and control your emotions. Now, take a step back from all the thought clutters and start to see how they fit together.

As you do so, you might realize that all thoughts, good or bad, all point toward the same thing. They all want you to become the best version of yourself. While some thoughts make you panic or worry about an upcoming event, they might point you to some flaws that you might need to address. Some thoughts that make you happy want to encourage you to work harder by showing you what you have accomplished thus far.

When you look at all your thoughts this way, you will realize that you might be panicking over nothing. Realizing that now means that you just made a very powerful move. It is choosing to pay attention to each passing thought or a choice to move in that awareness and to flow somewhere else entirely which is a little more distance away from those thoughts.

For now, just let the mind wander freely and acknowledge every thought that passes by.

(Pause 2mns)

No matter what you are thinking about, you may be overthinking it. The big problem you were stressing over a while back may not be that big a deal. Look back to the past to the moments when you thought you were in big trouble but things actually work out. You must have some of those moments in your life. In fact, your mind may be showing you that moment in your life now.

You know for a fact that you are much better than this. You already know that you are fully capable of handling whatever it is that life has to throw at you and come out on top at the end of the day.

The fact that you are worried means that there is something that is holding you back, something that can be removed. If so, what is it? Insecurity? Uncertainty? Many people have to deal with that, you know? They saw how they were lacking and yet they pushed through and they succeeded.

But let's take a moment to not look at the things that could go right. Instead of hoping that things go right, ask yourself what if things go wrong. What if you fail? What if it does not work out for you this time?

I want you to ask yourself "So what" after every "What if". If you fail, so what? You can always try again next time. Even if you cannot try it again, you will at least learn something from it that will help you improve. Even if it doesn't work out, there are other paths you can walk. It is never the end of the world when you fail. Even if it is the end of the world when you fail, you don't have to worry about anything else.

Maybe the failure itself is not so frightening. Maybe you are afraid of being criticized and ridiculed by your failure. Even if that is the case, you should not worry about that either. It is indeed painful to be laughed at, that much is certain. However, keep in mind that both your failure as well as the critics are equally and easily forgotten. Maybe it won't matter 3 months down the line. By then, you would look back at this situation and laugh, thinking that you should not have worried in the first place.

I want you to repeat this phrase to yourself a few times: "Even if worse comes to the worst, I can still cope." Repeat this to yourself for some time as you continue to observe the thoughts passing by.

(Pause 2mns)

At this point, all the clutters of thoughts should no longer trouble you as you have already taken a step back. You acknowledge their existence but refuse to get caught up in them. With this power, you can shut all of your thoughts out and focus on your own breathing because you know now that all the worldly worries are often more insignicicant than what you made them out to be.

Simply focus on your breathing and relaxing your body for a few more moments. I will now count to 10. As I count, bring your focus back to your body and the environment around you. I will now begin.

10… Slowly bring your focus back.

9… 8… 7…

6… Wiggle your toes and fingers now and feel how relaxed they are…

5… Rotate your shoulders a bit…

4… Take in a deep breath to tell your body that you are returning to the outside world.

3… Coming back to the outside world…

2… Start to move your body slowly and gently as if to shake each body part awake…

And 1… Slowly open your eyes and smile.

Relaxation Meditation (15mns)

Hello and welcome to this relaxation meditation.

To begin, find a quiet place with no distraction. That way, you can focus all your attention on relaxation. Sit however you want. If you are more comfortable lying down, go ahead and lie down. The key to a productive meditation session is comfort. Without it, relaxation cannot be achieved.

Once you are nicely settled in, we can get started. Simply take a deep breath to let your body know that it is time to unwind and relax. Take a deep breath in from your nose. Exhale through your mouth slowly, feeling the air flowing out.

Excellent. Now, do it a few more times, feeling yourself sinking deeper and deeper into relaxation every time. Let your body sink slowly into the state of tranquility, where no outside elements can disrupt your peaceful meditation session.

Continue to do this, allowing your body to relax and the breath to be the anchor to hold your mind in the present moment…

(Pause 2mns)

You should be thoroughly and fully relaxed. Allow your body to return to its original rhythm. Breathe as you normally would now.

At this point, there may still be thoughts that go through your mind. This is fine. This is natural. Simply observe your thoughts from afar, like an observer of your own thoughts, and refusing to get caught up in your own thoughts and emotions.

Do not beat yourself up for letting your mind wander, as this is a very natural thing. Even the most experienced people get distracted sometimes. Instead, just breathe in and enjoy every second you have with your own mind.

Whenever a thought comes to mind, simply acknowledge their existence. Perhaps, you could even observe them for a few seconds, but no longer. Push them away and return to your breath, using it as an anchor to hold your focus in the present moment.

Remember, you can always just come back to your breath after you have spent enough time with your breathing.

As you continue to breathe, give a color to the air that you bring into your body. Let's say that it has a bright blue color, the universal color for relaxation and energy. Feel this healing and relaxing aura filling you up. As you breathe out, feel this healing air going to all parts of your body and easing any tension in the body and anxiety in the mind.

Take a long and slow deep breath in through your nose. Move the breath all the way down into your abdomen, filling you up with light and making space. Allow your body to relax and let go. Allow your body to push away any negativity that might hold you back and weigh you down.

Continue breathing to allow your body to relax…

(Pause 2mns)

As you continue to breathe, remind yourself to stay with your breath. Think of it as an anchor to hold your mind in the present moment. If it starts to wander again, just gently guide it back to your breathing.

Right now, you are in complete control.

There is nothing you need to do other than staying with your breath and focusing on relaxing both the body and mind. There is a time and place for everything. Work and other things can wait.

This is your time. This is the personal time you make for yourself to rejuvenate. Give yourself permission to unwind, relax, and release all that pent-up negative energy. It is time to slow down and just unwind and relax.

Feel how deep and calm your breath has become. Continue to relax deeper and deeper.

You have been working so hard for so long. Your body is tired after all that ordeal. It needs peace and relaxation and you chose to give yourself these beautiful gifts to yourself. You chose to take the time out of your busy schedule to rejuvenate. What a wonderful gift you are giving yourself.

Feel your body becoming loose… More relaxed… More energized just from your breathing alone. This is the nourishment your body needs. Continue to breathe and relax…

(Pause 1mn)

As we come to the conclusion of this meditation, I will count to 10. As I do, slowly bring your consciousness back to your body, into the present moment…

1… You are slowly bringing your awareness back into your body.

2… Slowly bringing the comfort…

3… Slowly bringing the energy…

4… Slowly bringing the relaxation…

5… Back to the body…

6… Back to the mind…

7… You feel calm…

8… You feel at peace…

9… Now, slowly open your eyes.

10… You feel wonderful.

Depression Relieving Meditation (30mns)

Hello and welcome to this meditation to relieve depression and anxiety. At the end of this session, you will feel more at ease. You will feel calmer and better overall. To begin, get into a comfortable position. Sit or lie down however you want so long as you are comfortable in your position. Comfort is very important to a productive meditation session since you will be here for quite some time.

Right now, you don't even have to close your eyes. All you have to do is sit there and do some breathing exercises. Right now, you just have to create a natural breathing rhythm first before you really get into this session.

So let's start by taking 3 deep from the stomach.

In…. Slowly… And out…

In…. Slowly… And out…

In…. Slowly… And out…

Very good. Now, allow your eyes to gently close. No need to squeeze them shut. Just let them slowly fall and cover your eyes. As you do so, shift your focus to your own breathing. You may allow your breathing to return to its natural rhythm. Remain with your breath for a few more minutes.

(Pause 3mns)

As you continue to breathe, you may notice that your mind starts to wander. Maybe it'll bring up some really depressing things. Maybe it just brings up some random stuff. Whatever it is, simply disregard such thoughts.

Right now, there is nothing you need to do other than focus on your own breathing. Take it nice and easy and let your body loosen up. Continue to breathe as you were and let your body sink deeper into this state of relaxation.

(Pause 1mn)

You are grounded in the present moment. It accepts you exactly as you are right now. Feel the surface beneath your body. Surrender any holdings to it. Exhale, and let any tension flow out of you, out of your mind, out of your body, and allow a space to open up around you that's just for you.

Continue breathing from the diaphragm for another moment to let your body loosen up and sink deeper into relaxation.

(Pause 2mns)

Before you start to work on your own thoughts, take this moment to take care of your body first. You may not notice it, but your body is probably as damaged as your peace of mind. But this meditation will help you give your body the care it needs. I want you to scan your entire body from head to toe and notice any sore or tension in your body. Do it now while still breathing as you were.

(Pause 1mn)

Do you feel those tensions in your body? These may be the reason why you feel so down lately. So, we are going to fix that by soothing the pain of your body. Start by focusing your attention on the lowest point of tension and breathe deeply from the diaphragm.

As the air fills your lungs, imagine this air enveloping this point of tension and carry it out of your body as you breathe out. Continue to do this for the rest of your body until you no longer feel any tension in your body.

(Pause 2mns)

Now, take a few moments to think of what you have been feeling lately. Although depression has been overused, the fact remains that it is a very deep, dark, and dangerous place. It is a horrible place to be. No one, even you, does not deserve to be there. What you deserve is peace and happiness, not depression.

The world is indeed a cruel place, but you do not have to suffer alone. You are not hopeless. Others have been in this dark place before you. They had hope and they pulled through. You certainly will. Just have faith that all will be well. Believe that you are good enough and you will make something for yourself. Have hope and believe that everything will work well for you.

Now, take a step back and take a look into your past from another person's perspective. Ask yourself are you proud of the person you used to be? What about now? Maybe you are happy with yourself. Maybe you are not.

Even so, there is no point in denying your feelings. There is no right or wrong way to feel about something. All feelings are true and you should accept the fact that you are feeling down lately.

But there is hope. All the great people you admire all suffer from this emotional problem and they pulled through. Depression is real, but you do not have to suffer. You are not fated to endure this anymore. You are better than you think. You have the power to change your own fate.

So, stay here. Remain with yourself for a while and allow yourself to sink deeper into the state of relaxation. Put your attention into your breathing as it serves to anchor yourself to the present moment.

Now, as you continue to breathe, repeat these phrases to yourself.

"I am good enough."

"I am more than enough."

"I feel loved."

"There is nothing else I need to do right now."

"It is okay to be the way I am at this very moment."

"Things will be fine."

"All is well…"

"All will be well."

Remain with my words and let these truths sink in.

(Pause 2mns)

Everything almost always works out in the end. Sometimes, we worry over nothing. Sometimes, we just need to have some faith. The best thing you can do when things don't go your way is to do your best. Push forward. Go slowly if you need to. Rest if you cannot go forward.

Whatever you do, never ever give up. You are better than this. You know you are better than this. You know that you can pick yourself up and get yourself out of this problem. All you have to do is try and try again until you get better.

As you continue to breathe, take some time to reflect all the thoughts that are passing through your head. Some thoughts are pleasant. Others are not. Again, you do not need to deny your own feelings. No matter what they make you feel, all of the thoughts are there for a reason. They all want you to be the best version of yourself.

Some thoughts try to comfort and encourage you to do better. Other unpleasant thoughts just want to motivate you to do better through the pain. As you can see, all of these thoughts just want to encourage you to become the best version of yourself.

There is no self-hatred here. There is only self-love in action, just like parental love. One is kind and loving and the other is disciplined and tough, but all are love anyway. This is the same with the thoughts that cross your mind. Just acknowledge your thoughts and feelings and move on.

(Pause 2mns)

You deserve better. Much better than this. You have so much to live for. The world is a beautiful place and you deserve to enjoy this beauty. We are coming up to the end of this meditation. Repeat after me:

"It's okay to be just as I am in this moment."

"I am good enough."

"I am more than enough."

"I am greatly loved."

"I am supported."

"All is well…"

"All will be well."

To bring everything to a close, take three deep breaths now.

In… and out…

In… and out…

In… and out…

Stay here for as long as you like. When you are ready to return to the outside world, gently open your eyes.

Pre-Sleep Stress Reduction Meditation (15mns)

Hello and welcome to this pre-sleep stress reduction meditation. This is a guided meditation to help you relax after a long day. Start by finding a comfortable position. May it be on the floor or your bed, whatever is most comfortable for you.

Close your eyes and let your awareness go inward and your mind rest.

Sitting comfortably, placing your thumbs and index fingers together on each hand with your eyes closed, begin to focus on your breathing.

Inhale and exhale…

Inhale into your belly, feeling it expand outward and then exhale all the air out, allowing it to deflate.

Inhale into the rib cage, feeling the ribs move outward into space and letting all the air go and then a little bit into your ribs, then letting all of that air go from your ribs then from your belly.

Now, taking a deep breath into your chest, feeling it expand outward and then exhale all the air out, letting it go, combining all three together on your next inhale.

Starting from your belly, moving upward to your ribs, and then all the way into your chest, and then exhaling all the air out.

First from your chest, then your ribs, and then your belly, inhaling into your belly into your ribs, into your chest, then exhaling from your chest, ribs, and belly.

Inhale… Belly, ribs, chest, and exhale… Chest, ribs, and belly…

Feel any cool or warm sensations in your body as you breathe…

Inhale and let it go. As you continue your three-part breathing exercise, I want you to be the witness of your thoughts and see yourself going through your day today.

What you did this morning, what you ate, your interactions with others, the wide scope of emotions and experiences you might have had, the things you accomplished, and perhaps the things that you didn't.

You must realize that today is exactly what it was. The good or bad, whatever you think happened is over now and all is well.

Tomorrow, when you wake up, you are the creator of a brand new day. Today will be left behind and you can start fresh however you decide.

So, with this in mind let's introduce our mantra the centering thought for this meditation. Repeat after me…

"I move forward and leave today behind. I move forward and leave today behind…"

Repeat this message as you sink deeper into your meditative state. With each inhale, fill yourself with gratitude and fulfillment of what you accomplished today. With each exhale, let go of any negativity or self-judgment that you feel that may be lingering in your mind.

Let it go. You did your best and tomorrow is a fresh new start. Staying present with your breath.

Inhale… and exhale…

Allow each part of your face and body to sleekly let go and release… Again, chant with me…

"I move forward and leave today behind. I move forward and leave today behind. I move forward and leave today behind."

And now silently in your mind, it's time to release the mantra. Slowly begin to deepen your breath moving each finger, wiggling each toe at your own pace. Slowly begin to open your eyes or if you're ready for sleep to keep them closed and move to a lying down position.

Remember we are the creators of our own lives. We are in control of all energies in our lives using nothing but our own thoughts alone. If you have felt out of control in your life lately, stay with this mantra for the night or as you fall asleep to reassure yourself about your own inner power to move forward to whatever reality you desire every day is another chance at a fresh start and every night is a chance to leave behind whatever doesn't serve you.

Insomnia Meditation (20mns)

Hello and welcome to insomnia relieving meditation. To begin, get into a comfortable position. You can sit or lay down however you want so long as you are very comfortable. Comfort is of utmost importance after all.

At the end of this meditation, you should have a restful sleep. Before you close your eyes and dive deep into this sleep meditation, I want you to take a few deep breaths right now.

Breathe in…

And out…

In…

And out…

Once more. In…

And out…

You may close your eyes now. But do not squeeze your eyes shut. Simply allow the eyelids to come down slowly and naturally. For now, just focus on your bodily sensation and forget for the moment about trying to sleep.

Take a deep breath in, hold your breath at the top for a few seconds, then breathe out. Focus on how the air feels as it flows through your body. When you take control of your breathing, you also take control over your own mind.

Now, breathe as you normally would and be aware of how the air feels as you breathe. On your next breath in, feel the air going to your forehead. Let the cool air soothe the tension in that area… Relax… And let go…

On the next breath, feel your eyelids becoming softer and relaxed. Allow it to settle into its natural position. As you do, notice now your eyelids becoming heavier and heavier as they welcome sleep.

It is time to relax the body by soothing any sores and aches that are left. To do this, spend some time to observe your own body. Scan through every inch of your being as you continue to breathe naturally. Look for any tension or ache in your body.

Right now, you do not need to do anything about those aching areas. Just notice their presence and move on.

(Pause 2mns)

Now is the time to soothe those pain that makes your body feels uncomfortable. As you breathe in, imagine that this air brings with itself healing properties. Imagine this air flowing through your nose and soothing your entire body before gathering at the points of soreness.

Now, imagine that this healing energy goes to the areas of tension, wrapping around those areas, and soothing the tension as you exhale. Feel it fade away at each breath you take. Continue to do this for the rest of your body.

(Pause 3mns)

Now that the tensions in your body are gone, it is time we work on relaxing the rest of your body. On your next breath in, feel the cool energy to your cheeks and hold your breath. Exhale and feel your cheeks lower comfortably like they just drop deeper and deeper…

As you breathe in, focus on the muscles in your jaw area. Feel your teeth come apart and your lower jaw dropping slightly. Let your tongue rest at the bottom of your mouth, in its natural position. Focus on the muscles around your neck. On your breath in, feel the energy of that breath to knead away at your neck, taking the strain away.

On your next breath in, bring in a dose of relief to your back. The energy runs along your spine, unwinding all the knots in your upper and lower back. On your next breath out, allow any tension or aches to be carried away with it.

Feel your body sinking deeper and deeper into the state of relaxation. Bring your attention to your chest now and breathe in. As you do so, feel the air pulling apart all the knots that wind your chest up. As you exhale, savor the liberating relief of deep and satisfying relaxation.

Breathe in again and this time feeling your shoulders let go. They drop a little and the muscles in your arms your biceps and triceps and into the forearms. Feel any stress in this area melt away right down to the tips of your fingers.

Breathe in again and sending the breath right down to your abdomen and feel it expand and contract. As you breathe out, just letting it sink back in naturally and sending you into a deeper state of relaxation.

Now, harness the relaxing power of breathing and use its power to push the healing into your legs. Inject that energy and feel them relaxing and softening the muscles in your legs.

Upon breathing out, let any remaining pressure escape through the tips of your toes. Through the breath, you bring balance to your system. With each conscious breath, you become more and more aware of the present moment.

You are perfect. You are whole. Just take a moment now to observe the natural flow of your breathing. Notice how with each breath in, your chest rises, and with each breath out it falls.

Up and down just like the steadily swinging pendulum of life. Bring your attention to this precise moment, by simply coming back to your breath. You will return to the moment and become aware of it.

Just breathe in and then breathe out. Simply breathe in and breathe out again. And if something comes to mind, remain with the breath.

And now we will bring this meditation to a close. I will count you down from 10 and as I count down, sink deeper and deeper into a relaxed state.

10… Take the first step into the relaxation…

9… You are reminded of the soothing calmness of your breathing, letting go, surrendering…

8… Going down deep…

7… Breathing in and out drawing and closer to a blissful sleep

6… 5…

4… Breathe in and out, sinking deeper and deeper…

3…

2…

1… Spread your arms out wide and take one final deep breath in. As you breathe out, let yourself go completely into a profound and luxurious sleep that you deserve.

Deep Sleep Meditation (30mns)

Hello and welcome to this deep sleep meditation. It will help you fall into a deep and restful sleep. After this session, you will wake up feeling thoroughly relaxed and comfortable after getting a night of deep and restful sleep.

To begin, simply get into a comfortable position. As long as you are comfortable, you can put your arms and legs, however, and wherever you want. Comfort will be of utmost importance, after all. Since we will be here for a while, it is worth allowing yourself to be as comfortable as possible.

We will start with a simple breathing exercise. No need to close your eyes just yet. Simply take a deep breath in through your nose now, letting the air fill your lungs and stomach, hold it at the top, and through your mouth, your exhale goes.

Now, continue to breathe this way for another moment to allow your body and mind to settle into this meditation session.

(Pause 2mn)

During this time, you may notice that your mind starts to wander. This is totally fine. Our mind does this from time to time when it lacks stimulation from the outside world. It is used to be exposed to stimulants that it gets uncomfortable when there is peace and silence, even though they are good for the mind.

As you breathe, some thoughts drift through your mind about the things you did today or the things you need to do tomorrow. Some of them may remind you of something or someone. Certain thoughts might make you feel happy, sad, excited, or anxious.

That is all quite alright. You have been active your entire day, so you need something to help you unwind and relax. This is the moment to relax and to give your body and mind the rest they deserve.

Spend a few more minutes with yourself and just breathe and relax. Release all the tension from your body.

(Pause 2mns)

Now that your body is thoroughly relaxed, now is the time to clear your head so you can sleep. That way, you will wake up tomorrow refreshed and strong so you can handle your duties and roles. But, suppressing and not acknowledging their existence will only make it worse for you.

Instead, acknowledge their existence and feel everything you need to feel now so that you can get them out of the way and focus on the meditation at hand. Take a few moments to dwell on those thoughts before you sleep.

Rather than trying to forget those thoughts, focus on them. Feel what you need to feel. Think of what you need to think. For the next two minutes, do any worrying or thinking you think you should do. This is the time to clear your head.

(Pause 2mns)

From this point on, if your mind starts wandering, gently guide it back to the breathing. This is easy because you allow your mind to wander as much as it needs. Now, allow your breath to settle into its natural rhythm and blink slowly. Allow the weight of your eyelids to naturally curtain your eyes.

(Pause 2mn)

Now, scan through your body and notice any tension. Note how your body feels. Throughout this meditation session, you will focus on relaxing any tension in your body as well as calming the mind. Once your mind is restful, you can slip into a pleasant restful sleep.

Let us give the air a color: silver, to represent the purity of the air that you breathe in. The air that you are breathing now has the power to rid the body of any tension in your body. Air is one of the sources of life, after all. There is nothing better than to give your body as much as possible so it can start to relax and rejuvenate the body.

So, take a deep breath in, taking in the life-giving air and relax your body. Slowly exhale, letting the air carry any tension out from your body.

Right now, all you have to do is remain with your breathing and enjoy the relaxing sensation of your body. Right now, you just have to clear your head. Unwind, let go, and relax. That way, you will wake up the next day feeling very refreshed and energetic.

For that to happen, you need to relax. There is nothing else you need to do right now. Just be in the moment. Think of nothing but calm, relaxed thoughts. Notice how your body feels.

Even with this breathing, certain areas are still tense or sore. You may already notice them as you continue to breathe, but some sneaky ones bother you all the time, yet they elude you. Now is the time to locate them and work toward soothing the aches in your body.

So, I want you to scan through your body, starting from the head down to the tip of your toes. Notice how your body feels and note where the tensions and aches are. No need to do anything about them yet. Just acknowledge their existence. Start scanning your body now.

(Pause 2mns)

Now, let us work on soothing those areas. Let us give that pained area a color: red, to represent distress. Start with the area that is the tensest or sore. How does it feel? Focus on that area and breathe deeply. Imagine this silver air going into your body through your nose.

When you focus on that tense area, the magical and rejuvenating air goes straight to that area, caressing the aching area ever so gently, until the red area starts to lose its color and the silver air turns to light red. As you breathe out, the air that comes through your nose is light red and the pain starts to fade away.

Continue to do this for each area of the body until the tension in your body completely vanishes.

(Pause 2mns)

Now, note where your body feels more relaxed. Let us give this relaxation aura a color: greenish-blue, to represent rejuvenation and relaxation. Imagine that aura of relaxation spread throughout your body at each breath you take. Let this warm aura envelop your body and carry you in its magical cradle.

(Pause 2mns)

Remember that this relaxation and peace are not only limited to bedtime. With the same breathing exercise, you can bring this sense of relaxation and mindfulness with you throughout your daily life.

When the stress becomes unbearable, you can just step away from the problem. You can relax and take a break from the stress of life just by closing your eyes, recall the calming and relaxing sensation you are experiencing now, and breathe deeply and slowly.

When you do, your body will remember the meditation session that you chose to give yourself the day before. It will remember how to unwind when under stress. You can reclaim your peace of mind even when under stress. You are getting more than just a restful sleep. You are getting mindfulness, which is the most valuable gift you can give yourself.

Continue to breathe, relax, and enjoy this aura that envelops your body.

(Pause 2mns)

You are right where you want to be. There is nothing else you need to do other than to enjoy the tranquility of your mind and the relaxation of your body. You are making some personal time for yourself to relax and unwind after a long day.

You have been working hard all day. You deserve the rest. You deserve to have a restful sleep the moment your head hits the pillow up until the alarm rings. There will be no dreams or nightmares in-between to disrupt your sleep quality.

You will wake up, feeling strong, alert, and refreshed, ready to take on the next day's tasks with confidence, enthusiasm, and energy. You will do better in life, all because you choose to listen to your body and mind and give them the relaxation they need to function. So smile now and acknowledge the fact that you love yourself and give yourself the time to take care of your own body and mind.

Feel your attention drifting as you become calm and sleepy. For the next few minutes, you can choose to focus on counting and becoming more relaxed as you count. Concentrate your attention on number one.

As you count from one to ten, you will become more relaxed. As you loosen the tension in your body, you can let your mind drift into a pleasant, peaceful sleep. Start counting now.

1… Focus on number 1.

2… You are now more deeply relaxed. Let your body sink into a deeper, calm, and peaceful state.

3… Let the tension leave your body. Let relaxation fill your body and mind. Concentrate just on the numbers.

4… Picture that number in your mind. Relax, relax, relax. Let the tingly relaxation energy flow through your arms and legs. Feel how heavy but relaxed they've become. Dwell in this pleasant feeling.

5… As you drift deeper and deeper, embrace the relaxing aura. Let sleep wash over you. Let the peace wrap your entirety.

6… Relax…

7… Your body and mind are now very calm…

8… It feels pleasant and heavy…

9… Let your body drift deeper and deeper, floating in the protective aura.

10… You are now fully relaxed…

Now, you may start to count from 10 back to 1. When you reach 1, you will be fully relaxed and can drift into a deep sleep. Start counting when I say start. Slowly count as I talk. Focus only on the numbers as I speak.

Start now at 10, and count down. Focus slowly on each number as you count and keep going on your own.

As you are becoming more deeply relaxed… Feel the warmth… Heavy… Comfortable… Peaceful….

Relax… Drifting asleep… Drifting… Pleasant and calm… Accepting… Relax… Sleep… Pleasant and peaceful…

At peace with yourself… Nurturing… Relax… Calm and quiet… Deep relaxation and sleep… Quiet…

Slow, even breathing… Calm… Warm… Relaxed… Peaceful… Let yourself drift into a deep sleep… Deep, pleasant sleep… Sleep… Thank you and goodnight.

Sleep Hypnosis 1 (90mns)

Hello and welcome to this sleep hypnosis. To begin, make sure that you are in a place where you can safely relax, in a place free from distractions. Then, give yourself all the conscious permissions to deeply and completely enjoy and benefit from this session in your own way.

You might already feel the urge to close your eyes after feeling that familiar relaxation wave washing over you just as you gave yourself permission to relax. So let us take advantage of this relaxation wage. Go ahead and lay your head down on your pillow and signal to yourself that it is now entirely okay to take those first few delightful steps to move gently deeper down into the waiting promises of that inner peacefulness within.

But first, let us go ahead with a simple breathing exercise to relax the body further. Just remain wherever you are and you don't have to close your eyes yet. You can let them wander however they like for now. So go ahead and take a deep breath now.

Excellent.

Now, in through your nose, breathe in using your diaphragm, letting the air completely fill your lungs. Then, through your mouth, let the air out slowly and feel the air exiting your body.

Excellent. Now, continue to breathe like this for a few minutes.

(Pause 1mn)

Excellent. Now, just go ahead and close down those eyes and with the eyes closed down, and you are comfortable listening along to the sound of my voice, it may be helpful to you to remember that, as my voice goes deeper with you, if something or anything should happen during this restful experience anything that requires your immediate outside attention, then no matter how deeply you do relax if your external situation requires it, you'll always be able to quickly and easily open those eyes and return again to your fully alert state attending to whatever may be needed.

But for these moments now, I'd like you to just let go as best you can of the distractions of your outside world and begin to enjoy these senses of your own, developing an internal world and you can encourage yourself to relax a little more into a restful comfort by saying to yourself this mantra quietly within your own thoughts:

"I am now choosing to enter into a state of healthy pleasant and deep relaxation. And even in relaxing, I know I always remain within all choices of my own control. I am here learning how to let go of exactly the level of calmness and relaxation."

You may be finding yourself relaxing a little more already just by telling yourself and acknowledging those words. You may begin to discover that, as you do move a little further into your peaceful awareness, it's often much easier to notice those other non-visual sensors within us.

Those other sensors in our body start to heighten as we turn our attention inward to our bodies. They will become a bit more in tune with the body, more noticeable, and perhaps even more interesting if you have not spent much time observing your body. These things start to become very noticeable when the eyes are closed.

For example, you may soon become aware of some different sounds that you may be hearing around you. You may notice the smell of the air through the nose. You might taste something as you rest your tongue at the bottom of you. It may be the touch and sensations of the surfaces underneath you which brings your awareness to those points of contact where your head or your back or your legs meet and touch and connect with the comfortable sheets or a mattress below.

And for a few moments here, I want you to just let yourself check in with your physical senses without any judgment or any need to analyze or any need to do anything at all. Just taking a calm note of whatever sensations may be experienced in this present and allow any subtle changes to also occur, noticing that as the body does rest and relax sensations come and go and continue to change and develop becoming different from moment to moment and second to second.

(Pause 1mn)

And after a short while of this awareness, your mind may very likely also begin to drift or it may wander about in some ways because you know it really is the nature of our minds to so often search out for a new focus, or to bring up random thoughts all those spontaneous ideas, or perhaps seeking out certain words or phrases almost as if there were a type of dialogue inside of yourself where one part of you is wanting to speak and another part of you is wanting to listen.

Speaking and listening within yourself in this way, we may find there are certain images, pictures, or glimpses of flashing details, which the thinking mind may wish to replay a recall just like scenes from your own personal films or photographs or snapshots from your past from your most immediate and recent day.

I'd like you to just allow this familiar process of the thinking mind wandering about to very deliberately and consciously now occur. So, if you find the thinking mind wants to jump up and down in some energetic way or it wants to compete for your better attention from the words you are hearing, then you can just let that happen for this little while.

If the mind wants to steer that awareness towards some particular meaning or some particular picture or some language of ideas, go ahead now and give it every permission to go there for the mind to just move wherever and however it will.

I know this may seem to you a little contradictory to make this kind of choice here at first, but just remember it's very important to let the thinking mind know that, yes, it does have an important purpose to you and yes, the thinking-self can be acknowledged and it can be heard.

The deeper you do go, the more your observational-self now really can begin to step back a little and to realize and it also has a powerful choice. A choice which is to pay attention to each passing thought or a choice to move in that awareness and to flow somewhere else entirely, which is a little more distance away from those thoughts.

After a few more moments of allowing the thinking self to be entirely at play, I'd like you to allow your focus to gently change a little more just by consciously directing it gently and slowly towards your own breathing.

So, go ahead now and take in a few deeper breaths three or four more deliberate breaths now by breathing in through the nose, and then out through the mouth and notice the rise and fall of your chest and your stomach.

Notice how the body naturally relaxes again a little deeper each time with each breath. Now, allow the breath to return to its natural flow. Just allow your breathing to return to its natural cycle. Notice that your breath has its own natural flow similar to that of the flow of thoughts you just experience.

As you acknowledge this, you become more and more observant over this time of the natural cycles of each thought noting how each thought can arrive, and then each thought can go, discovering that there is always a kind of beginning a middle and an end to each passing thought.

These can be more clearly observed if you just make a little more room to do so. Now even in this very simple way, you may already be finding that some of the more compulsive urgencies that so often come with the habits of excessive or chronic thinking are already beginning to dissipate.

The impulses carried with each passing thought may also be losing some of their strength or potency because the more that your observational-self understand that these thoughts can come and go just like the passing comets o meteors flashing and disappearing in the vastness of the space of your mind, the further you can start to relax into those broadening spaces and move a little more to wherever those disappearing thoughts eventually fade away.

When they do trail off and disappear, you may choose to stop this recording here if this already suits your needs because you may already feel this is enough to allow you to let go of all thinking as you do move into your best and refreshing sleep.

But if you have a feeling that you would like to go a little deeper down into an even deeper comfort and calm relaxation, then in just a few moments, I'm going to ask you to do something a little less usual.

(Pause 1mn)

I'm soon going to invite you to move in a slightly different way just moving away from this meditative or mindful type of space by beginning to orient yourself more and more towards a deeper hypnotic style of space.

If you would like to try this, then in just a few short moments, I'm going to ask you to very soon open your eyes once more. This might very well be the key to your relaxation as you will enjoy this powerful result that can come by learning how to develop and deepen your calmness even more as you learn some of these powerful techniques of self-hypnosis.

So, go ahead now and open your eyes once more. As your eyes do open, perhaps completely or perhaps only to halfway, notice how those eyes there may already be searching for something new to focus or look upon.

So give your eyes now a point of focus for them to view by selecting a random spot somewhere in front of you, or just choosing a small detail of any interest up there on the wall, or find a random little spot somewhere up on the ceiling you can notice the size and the colorings of that certain spot.

That's all you have to do for these few seconds of holding the eyes open until the eyelids are now blinking more and more and with each blink, they are growing heavier and heavier. So much heavier over time that it really is a struggle to keep them open now and the lids themselves are so droopy and drowsy. It's as if a powerful magnet is drawing them together and that powerful force is becoming impossible to resist.

(Pause 2mn)

When that happens, stop trying to look at all and stop trying completely and feel the eyes relaxed as they do come down again, allowing them to close now with a reassuring and solid nod. The important part here to remember is to immediately give yourself this simultaneous suggestion:

"As my eyes closed down, I go deeper and deeper. As my eyes closed down I go deeper and deeper."

You can use this hypnotic command for yourself to very quickly relax yourself right before you go to bed. You can it in this way and right away now so you can also strengthen and expand your relaxation by using your creative mind's eyes. We are going to use the power of the creative mind to create a place of peace and tranquility for the mind and soul.

Now, just imagine a picture and feel a special kind of wave-like energy. Something wonderful like the smooth flow of honey or a magic elixir of sorts. Something which slowly sends a healing balm like the essence of pure tranquility down.

Now from behind those closed eyes as you feel that elixir passing through all of your body, soothing you like a gel from the inside out and your wave of calmness may flow in your favorite color or it may descend with soft and gentle vibrations or it may take you deeper and deeper with gentle tingles. Now of coolness or warmth, or it may soften you with an accompanying sound or a tranquil song, whatever it is you imagine.

It's all to your benefit to trance yourself in this calming way. So just take this time to enjoy this sense of serenity unfolding and cascading now inside of you like the lap of a silvery moonlit tide, calmly washing its pure foaming waves over to smooth the softening sand below as you experience your facial features relaxing.

Feel the tensions ease away from the forehead and the scalp your cheeks, in your jaw muscles, loosening down along your neck. The stiffness there is receding and old tensions or burdens held across your shoulders are lifting and dissolving all tightness is loosened away from the chest and the chest muscles expand to open with ease into your diaphragm and down along your arms.

It is feeling better and better to loosen and let go feeling the elbows loosen your wrists in your hands and your fingers stretching out to find their full and natural length and down the length of your spine. The wave is passing each part of your back and every vertebra is finding its natural release. It's almost as if these sensations are so familiar to you just like putting on a cozy and familiar jacket or coat that you love so much.

You are wrapping relaxation around you entirely as the stomach releases all tensions held there dispersing to settle your digestive system as the serene wave melts into your hips and washing away all tensions from you, from the very center of your body now, reducing and melting away so many old stresses as the thigh muscles lengthen, the knees unlock and the carves are loosening.

Your lower legs are finding so much more comfortable as their ankles give up all previous tensions and the more you relax now, the better you feel because the better you feel, the deeper you continue to go, allowing soothing waves into the balls and the soles of the feet all the way to the very tips and ends of your toes.

It's as if your entire body now is being massaged by expert hands. The magical hands which melt away every last ounce of physical tension or tightness that might remain. Now, because you are so deeply relaxed and you are breathing so freely and deeply it's fine for the conscious mind to wander off however it will or for your thoughts to move away and back again.

Just make sure to come in touch now and then as you understand the meanings that come with each of my following words. In reality, the unconscious mind often takes over in every session like this one. It's your unconscious mind that is much more interested to hear, to listen, and better align you to orient yourself so much further down towards those important goals of your original purpose.

It's your unconscious self that knows most of all how to positively and powerfully change what has bothered you until now. What has been bothering you way back there when you first began and decided to make these changes just by listening to these words, how best to resolve everything that has preoccupied your thinking mind in those ways up until discovering these moments of improving clarity and improving the sense of clearing your thoughts.

Because here it is that you are now learning how to adjust in your very own thinking patterns and how to best continue in clearing your mind in your positive days and nights ahead by permanently improving your own habits of a clearer mind to adjust all of the deeper settings and deepest programming dials down at that deepest core level.

(Pause 1mn)

I want you now, in your unconscious imagination, to continue to expand, to explore, and to freely connect upon and associate to these ideas as you build deeply towards wherever you truly connect inside of yourself the most to arrive at the place of your creative and best new solutions and to go there now.

This is the place where your own wisest knowledge speaks to you, talking back to you with such powerful words. So go there now by moving in this way just like descending down a long circular set of stairs where you can see and sense a vast and open ancient library awaiting you below, or you may choose to move through a beautiful shining portal stepping through doorways of the light.

You're going down and down now as you step and move into the very basement of your total and absolute consciousness, until finally after some time, you do arrive at your lowest floor. This is the lowest floor of your relaxation as you decide to open those large and sturdy doors awaiting you.

You discover yourself now stepping and choosing to move into your truest and most authentic place of power where you are ready to receive all of your own most powerful insights.

Now as you arrive and feel yourself tuning into the powerful aura of this place. You feel the absolute vastness and the infinite potential of your currents of deep learning and you see yourself here perhaps even dressed in a special way perhaps dressed in beautiful or ornate ancient robes or in a way that you choose as you easily walk and drift and float and directly take the form of your wisest highest being.

Step in now to that shape made apparent from your core-self, this shape of your higher-self because in this form, you are now ready and open to receive these important new messages which can all be now deeply understood and deeply absorbed and acted upon exactly when you choose.

As you take this time to look about you, you find yourself in your own infinite halls of power and you realize before you hanging on one of these walls there is an equally powerful pure crystal mirror.

So, you move over to see. There, a stunning reflection which shines back to you so many images of your own very best ideals and clear-self, and upon closer inspection, you now allow yourself to look into all of those hidden aspects and those hidden parts of yourself that were previously resistant to change.

You are beginning to understand now so much more with a more comfortable clearer view you and even if you choose, you know you may reach out to place your hands into that silvery surface to directly and permanently change whatever you wish to change within you by your own hands and your own power.

Begin to do that now, reaching out and changing as you continue to gaze calmly and clearly upon your own habits of the mind. You reach out and into that mirrored surface which becomes like an accepting fluid or a liquid which can also powerfully shape and bring you new solutions.

These new solutions are for every positive change to your habits of thinking that you are now deciding to make now. It's almost a special kind of profound revelation to realize with new eyes how your own mind can hold its pockets of tightness or constrictions or tensions just like the muscles and tendons and nerves of the physical-self.

There are frustrations, obstacles, worries, and concerns that can be held in the mind which often become stuck there into patterns that repeat themselves with leftover energies. Some of those unwanted thoughts become itched into a kind of loop, stuck like a needle on an old-time record player playing the same snippets of songs over and over and over again. Even though that tune has been heard far too many times, it sometimes takes a simple hand to reach in and reposition that record player's needle to continue on to the rest of the path.

Just as a wise teacher once taught, the more we try to hold on to this thought, or that what we try to cling on to this idea or that, the more the mind tries so hard to plan every detail or to go over and over for the hundredth time. The more we try to recall certain events from the previous or past day or even days before, the more the mind overworks in this way, the more tired and the more tiring it becomes to the rest of our being, just like a muscle working too hard to hold on to a great weight after too long.

The muscle simply needs to loosen and relax its grip to release and settle back again into a time better spent in absolute recovery and clearing to a more restful blank slate. You know there is so much more pleasant to be gained with that relief by remembering we are so much more than not only our muscles and nerves but by knowing you are so much more than even your thoughts knowing at the end of each day, it really does feel much, much healthier to unwind in the mind, to unwind into an easier natural night's sleep simply by releasing those weights and letting go of that grasping.

Just as your head feels that comfortable pillow beneath, you know the mind does learn its cue and it does know how to relax, how to clear, how to rest just as you are remembering now. But when you wake again tomorrow, all of those thoughts, if you choose them, will still be there, ready and waiting to join you again with such a renewed positivity. It's almost becoming impossible not to smile at that realization which feels so incredibly good to know that you know now how to clear your mind.

(Pause 1mn)

You might already know how your clearest mind came especially by listening in to a quieter inner voice inside of you. You may know how you permanently turn down that old style of the minds that has too much chatter, to a more comfortable level by reducing that volume to where it no longer concerns you.

Maybe with those thought volumes reduced, you now see how you learned your deepest lessons by reaching out in a new way. To trust in your rich treasure troves inside by unlocking those chests and connecting to those richer parts of you that really do reassure you with so much calm confidence and strength of clarity.

As you look back upon yourself, you let yourself know that, yes, you really do deserve to be calm at this moment, and yes, you really can be so self-assured without constantly holding on to this thought of that because it feels so much better inside of yourself to know you made all of your own decisions to finally let go completely.

As you relaxed into a clearer mind and the best sleep just like right now, and maybe your sleepiest-self is now hearing these other messages and seeing so many other peaceful sublime tranquil images with their own types of soothing feelings and relaxing sounds, which really do make you feel entirely rested and refreshed so deeply within.

Because your sleeping mind now understands that all of those problems that were once carried for far too long can also be put down now and forever released for this more comfortable while to take such a load off forever from your sleeping mind.

That's a powerful choice to see now reflected in that special crystal mirror and I don't think my voice needs to remind you for much longer of that simple bedtime fairy tale where the wisest prince and the wisest princess succeeded in their clear-mindedness simply by deciding not to try anymore just like all of those times when you really didn't have to try so hard did you to rest and recover and relax into a clearer night's sleep because there was no real effort required to do that.

So, allow yourself to let go of the day, to rejoice in exploring so many positive and pleasant dreams, floating away with such bliss to always be coming over those clearer shores, freely expand and explore what it can mean to take flight into the sublimity of the beyond.

Very soon, you realize when you go about your following days, that tomorrow, and the days after, you are seeing and knowing yourself as someone who is no longer weighed down by so many troubling thoughts because you are seeing and feeling and knowing yourself to be so much clearer in your mind

This feels so good to integrate and accept all of these meanings to truly live and rest and sleep now, completely in this deeply relaxing way. So, as you do take your flights of fancy dreaming ahead with such grace and ease, you may find yourself moving up and away into the clearest night skies or even further up to higher and higher to ascend into the atmospheres above you.

This magical place is where even the shining stars now welcome you into all spaciousness beyond, embracing your sleeping form. Now, as you journey with your sleeping-self toward a night of deep, peaceful, and restful sleep, to rest, to rejuvenate, and to replenish, you sleep with such calmness and such happiness. You may even begin to glow on the inside with a newly found innate, pure, clear, and calm joy. And now you are drifting away entirely and do your very best sleep and so I wish you good night.

Sleep Hypnosis 2 (90mns)

Hello and welcome to this hypnosis for deep relaxation and peaceful sleep. To begin, get into a comfortable position, be it laying down or sitting up, whatever works for you. Comfort is of utmost importance for relaxation and sleep, after all.

First, we will start off with a simple breathing exercise. So go ahead and take a deep breath now.

Good.

In through your nose, hold it at the top for a few seconds, and out through your mouth.

Excellent.

Now, do that for a couple of minutes. Right now, you don't even have to close your eyes or focus on anything in particular. Right now, just focus on breathing like this to tell the body that it is time to unwind and relax.

(Pause 2mns)

Now, you can start by signaling to both your body and your subconscious mind by letting their eyes close down and welcoming that gentle change of focus. Shift that focus on your breathing as the curtains of the eyelids descend.

You know that great sleep awaits you as you feel it wrapping around your eyelids in its own cloaks of that soft velvety dim as the space here behind your eyes becomes just a little more curious and maybe your physical self that relaxes the most first before your deeper mind begins to follow moving the body just a little here or there. Give your body some time to adjust to the mattress and relax.

Feel the enjoyment and relief as you feel every muscle lengthen in relaxation. Feel that relaxation behind your closed eyes as the muscles in your cheeks and jaw loosen. They allow you to unclench those teeth or perhaps you're moving your waist or your back a little easier to one side or another.

We might like to stretch out a left shoulder or lower down the right and there's often a pleasing sensation like an unclasping or detachment from stress and discomfort that begins to ripple on down and travel with soft vibrations or enjoyable tingles like soothing cycles of tranquil waves relaxing you over time more and more.

Feel this relaxation inside as the muscles of the face do soften and any lines across the forehead to smooth and flatten out. It's comforting in ways to know that we really do continue to move a little deeper into relaxation even from each passing moment to moment as we journey positively through to a peaceful and restful sleep.

Just as you can become aware of your breathing and relaxation you now although it may slow or calm down your chest and your stomach continue to gently rise and then fall because your relaxing body is always in some sort of rhythm of easy automatic streaming cycling through these repeating calming motions even within the deepest of deep sleep.

Take a moment and enjoy this relaxation now because these natural rhythms are constant. As constant as the passing seasons and this process of change is continual. Even if it's much easier to often just forget to take a deeper breath to allow you to relax more and more, each exhale allows you that chance for an even greater possibility for relaxation.

You may become aware of your breathing over time as it is aligning powerfully for you aligning more and more to this relaxing state of self-changing and transforming you positively towards deep sleep. Whenever you choose to create those special patterns of a circadian circle and very soon or whenever you do choose to, just breathe out a little more slowly you know you'll be making all conscious decisions to unconsciously let yourself go.

As this happens, there may come a new awareness, stirring like a pleasing rush of sensations and awareness of deeply restful waves, washing through you and passing into you with all of this rejuvenating calm as a type of clearing decompression may bring you pictures or images of so many well-oiled but overly winded springs.

You could imagine those springs all releasing one after the other. Of course, they must do so over time to unwind and expand to reset and it feels so good here to begin uncoiling just like that to uncoil and unwind and de-stress within.

Trust in your deeper powers to relax and allow yourself to sink deeper into relaxation with great satisfaction as you better trust in your own sleep's control knowing that this decision right now is making it easier and easier to just better let go.

You know now is your right time to set aside all cares to release the day's pent-up energies and set down those older washed-down ideas. Leave all outdated wakeful concerns behind you somewhere or wherever it may be because instead now you're choosing to move deeper and move a little further away traveling easily and dreamily from wherever it is.

Those conscious daytime thoughts will now go and it feels so good and so right to unconsciously watch this happened from afar to picture passing thoughts now playing out from this more objective distance as you begin to see the thinking mind tiring itself out.

It might even be a little amusing for you to be witnessing all thoughts arriving just as soon as they inevitably disappear and then go like flashes of bright comets that may burn brightly momentarily in the vast darkness of your vision.

You see they're fading away again soon as quickly as shooting stars. The energies of each thought dimming and leaving trials across a clearing majestic night sky. It may be your unconscious mind already knows how to better fade and float all thoughts away, clear away those remnants of awaking mind now, past business now, to reset permanently this new canvas of the resting minds.

It's so much more pleasing and interesting to remember and recall that a good night's sleep is only natural to you and a perfect night's sleep is really your true and natural birthright. As you move down and glide down and so many undisturbed and always more pleasing ways always, you're moving deeper here into sleeps welcome sanctuaries, connecting and orienting unconsciously, to your own private secluded retreat, just like when you were younger way back in those earlier years and there were those times when you most enjoyed so many delightful little naps.

It's like sinking backward further and further toward relaxation because you are doing that right now, relaxing in the way that allows you to soothe the mind, body, and soul. You can find this relaxation as easily just by recalling this sense of peace and tranquility.

You're finding your subconscious mine now and it automatically orients you towards sleep more and more every time. If I were to say to you that word "sleep" right now you might also be choosing to allow the very sound and the sense of this healing type of word to encourage you only deep inhale, moving you much, much further down beyond our every level of the previous relaxation you've enjoyed and felt so far.

It can be like seeing or imagining so many thousands of soft granules of sand. As you picture those tiny sand grains falling and dropping down through an old-fashioned hourglass, you can watch them fall so beautifully down to spiral and rest and settle.

They're all the way at the bottom where your deeper-self now sits because you're melting and dissolving all tensions away and always returning yourself into this serene place and its oasis and these other loveliest times when you're just drifting and traveling, just being at ease and floating inside through all passing and pleasing interior dreams while these idyllic senses and idyllic scenes of your own personal event can lay you back into all spaciousness.

Parts of you know it's a thrill to surf within your own mind gliding and floating across all slowing crests of so many peaceful dream waves because you're choosing this time to sleep now. You know you're confident inside to enjoy your very best relaxation.

You now reset your own inner clock and this is making it easier for you to remember when you sleep. As you are continuing to nourish the body with relaxation and tranquility, I want you to hear me now using the power of the subconscious mind. Tune in to my relaxing words and positive suggestions. The subconscious mind will do the rest for you.

Always know and remember that you are entirely free to fall asleep exactly now or at any moment you choose because there's always so much time for you to sleep as the dreamy wings of your special fantasies can transform your daydreams into your magical nights dreams of total peace in this space.

This place where beautiful dreams take place, where relaxation is the rule, and where the mind, body, and soul rejuvenate. You are in such a special place where and now as you float and step into beauty connected into true peacefulness and the deepest calm and you're feeling perfectly safe and serene because you feel empowered and protected.

You know there's no one around here no other can see within your fields. As you wander and drift happily by yourself, you're discovering what it's like to float out across so many horizons always in such soothing and sublime ways, floating now as you step out and floating through all spaciousness.

Very soon, I want you to see a beautiful clearing type of you as magical dream doors open wider and you realize that you are in a very magical place. You realize that you are standing at a stunning beachside cove. You're enjoying the sights and the sound of this tranquil seaside by this untouched heaven of purity that you see. Now here before you, and from this safe vantage point way up high, you realize you're looking out and widely across an enormous horseshoe-shaped cove because you're witnessing the stunning beauty of this tropical paradise so radiant and vibrant with no earthly equal.

You're looking out so far now across a great blue and green tranquil sea gazing across the calm, clear waters and enjoying the most placid silvery ocean that you've ever seen. Because everything here is so peaceful and everything here seems to naturally glow expanding with an aura of calm to reach out and touch you, it's like a slow-moving oil painting as if all the pretty colors and oils seem to blend and merge into something so deeply relaxing.

You see the palm trees all swaying as you feel the cool seaside breeze brushing against the soft skin of your face where you take these moments to inhale and smell the clearing sense of this fresh air as a refreshing saltiness of the sea wind relaxes you even more.

You breathe in total healing as this health cascades and flows down through your lungs. It's like a wash of reassurance and renewing strength expanding all of your self-belief and all of your self-worth into every deepest fiber of your soul. And now, you find yourself moving down again down a set of floating moving stairs because you're hovering now down to that beachhead below.

You're moving down and down to touch down to those waiting sands there until you feel your heel and the soles of your feet sinking and melting into this welcoming carpet of pure health as you spread out and relax every one of your toes you feel you're being called forward now with new and easier steps.

Up ahead, in the distance, you are seeing a floating hammock or a comfortable-looking bed there just resting and looking so perfectly comfortable. Tell yourself that it is perfectly safe and secured as it rests between two tall and sturdy-looking palm trees.

Very soon, you're aware of lowering and sinking yourself down, with each step through that sand, as you move on and on towards that bed until you find yourself sinking down and resting into the comforts of that bed, down into the luxuriance of this perfect waiting court, as you feel yourself lying down and relaxing underneath the cooler leafy shade of these tall sturdy trees, as you see them sway so gently in the breeze.

You're lazing back now feeling your body sinking even more in to enjoy the perfect cushioning and the supple and soft support underneath you as you arrest more and more and truly lie back. And little by little now, as you drift into sleep, you're allowing the soft rolling sound the nearby peaceful waves to lower you into even deeper levels of the deepest calm.

As every new silver crested wave washes and breaks on that shore, you feel yourself expanding and experiencing the most incredible deepest relaxation you could ever know. As you enjoy your perfect floating hammock, beginning to rock you now so gently in the breeze, from side to side, rocking in perfect time with each new splashing wave, you know in your deepest mind and awareness.

You only continue to carry yourself through this session with all serenity. As you begin to look out and explore ahead across your many coming days and into every restful mind yet to come, you know you'll remember how easy it is for you to go to sleep because you see yourself falling asleep.

So, you quickly and entirely on your leisure just as soon as you feel your head touching down to that pillow, you know you'll be asleep and simply and as naturally as taking in a deeper breath. Just as you do right now, continuing to just rest and breathe because your sleep-self is now resting and resetting over this time. Allow your dreaming mind to be free, untethered, to float and wander to any beautiful experiences that you fancy as all happiness falls into you to relax.

As you dream more and more with all peaceful joy, rejuvenating and repairing yourself automatically, your healing spirit is recharging and naturally repairing you organically and powerfully, or just sleep now as you continue to relax. Just sleeping and sleeping because they taped down. You know now is the perfect time to swing as you fall so easily into a deep and complete natural sleep.

Thank you and goodnight.

Bedtime Stories for Adults 1 (90mns)

Once upon a time, there was a village at the foot of a tall and mighty mountain. In that village lived Leo. It was Leo's birthday and while he was working in the rice field, his friend Dave shouted over him to come quick.

Sensing the urgency in his friend's voice, Leo darted to the edge of the village, where he saw a tall red light surrounding the village. People called it the death barrier and that anyone who dared to step beyond it will inevitably die. But its existence has been long established.

The urgency was that of his father, who lied motionless beyond the barrier. Leo's heart skipped a beat at the sight and he went beyond the barrier to his father, who was no longer breathing by the time Leo got to him.

Leo dragged his limp body back to the village, away from the barrier. The village doctor arrived and checked his father over. The doctor sighed and shook his head, his lips thinned, a dejected look.

"I am sorry, son," The doctor said, "He is dead."

Leo's heart stopped for a moment. It took him a while for his brain to register these words, let alone the fact itself.

"The Chimera did this, as to many of those who stepped over the barrier."

The next day, the village folk visited Leo's house to attend his funeral. They all said something along the line of, "Isn't it a shame…", "Sorry for your loss", and so on and so forth. Leo thanked them for their visit. The neighbors kept him busy and made him forget about his farther momentarily, but it was not too long until Leo was all alone again.

Leo was not used to being alone and he hoped he'd get good at being alone soon. Later that night, he sat next to the window and gazed upon the great mountain that glowed with the light and savagery of what the villagers referred to as the New Gods.

Leo wondered what the gods were doing up there.

When Leo slept, he dreamt of the malevolent Chimera that took his father away from him. He dreamt of its piercing eyes that were full of rage, malice, and pride. He dreamt of this beast's shadow that loomed over the village perpetually, causing the villagers endless suffering for hundreds of years, bringing nothing but misery.

And now, it was Leo's father's turn to be at the mercy of this beast.

Enough is enough, Leo thought to himself.

Leo got up before sunrise, packed some food and water into a satchel, and went to the pyre where his father had been cremated. Leo took his father's ashes and put them into a jam jar. With all the items he needed, Leo sauntered toward the edge of the village, where the death barrier stood.

Just before he passed that red line, someone yelled at him.

"Stop!"

It was the village doctor.

"If you take another step forward, you will die. Leave the Chimera alone. There is no way you could win against that beast."

But those words fell on deaf ears. Leo took a deep breath and walked over the red line, into the forest ahead. He walked all day long, looking for the beast, but found nothing. As he walked, he saw his father's face in the trees. As he walked, he wondered where had his father gone.

It was kind of cruel of his father, Leo thought, a man who'd given him his time and love, and taught Leo how the world worked. The man had brought Leo breakfast in the mornings and blankets in the evening. The man was his father and he bought Leo up to be the man that he was today.

And now, that man was forever gone. He had gone off into the darkness, leaving Leo all alone. He did not even get the chance to bring his father breakfasts in the mornings and blankets in the evening. Leo could not bring his father back. All of this was because of the Chimera, that beast.

Leo was determined to slay that beast himself. Though it may not bring his father back, Leo would make that beast pay for what he had done to his father and all other villagers that came before him.

Leo's out of water and thirsty thanks to the rage that boiled within him. He spied the great mountain above the trees and walked towards it. At the foot of the mountain was a river, so clear he wouldn't know the water was there if it did not reflect the sunlight. The water was cool and Leo drank from the river for a long time.

When he was done, he wiped his lips and looked up. There stood an old lady who sat on the rock a few feet away from him. In her hand was a hip flask from which she took a swig. Leo ignored the old lady and turned to leave, wondering where he should look for the beast next.

Just as he did so, the old lady yelled.

"Hey! I've seen a large Chimera coming by earlier. You sure you want to be out here all alone?"

Leo stopped. "What do you know about this beast?"

The old lady described the beast to Leo. She said that the beast stood tall, as big as an ox, with large and mighty dragon wings, and a purple snake for a tail that can spit venom. It did sound dangerous, but Leo was not afraid.

She pointed up the mountain. "I saw him! Went that way, he did."

"Did he now?", Leo said.

"Oh yes! And a mighty smug look he had about him also."

"Yeah."

Leo began to walk away. Just as he did, the old lady told Leo that that was where the beast lived. She said that it lived in the mountains, where it would plot and scheme and think of his evil plans for the poor villagers.

"And he said something about having just killed an old man. He must be your father, hm?"

"Indeed. Well, that was beyond coincidence", Leo thought. "Maybe she knew something."

And with this new destination in mind, Leo started off for the mountain instead.

The old lady yelled again, something about taking her with him, but Leo ignored her.

He walked for an hour or so. Then, he saw another figure ahead up the mountain, sat on the ground. It was the same old lady, again. Leo was dumbfounded. There was no way she could catch up to him like this.

"How did you get here?" Leo asked. The old lady shrugged and took another swig at her hip flask.

"You'll need a guide around these parts," She said, "That beast is difficult to kill, you know that right?"

Leo sighed and said, "Listen, I don't want to be mean or anything… But you look drunk, old, frail, and quite useless, really. How much can you help me in my quest to kill this beast?"

"Wow. You are being rude", she said.

Leo walked on, but she followed behind. She told Leo that she knew many things, such as the beast and the New Gods.

"You're delusional," Leo responded. But the old lady insisted on coming with him. She promised Leo that she would show him how he could slay that beast, to which Leo scoffed.

"I'll kill that thing with my bare hands if I have to," Leo said.

This elicited a laugh from the old lady.

"Don't be silly. You won't kill that thing with your bare hands."

And so the two climbed the mountains and looked everywhere. They looked in caves and every crevice they could find, but the Chimera was not there. That thing must've gone further up, and so they scaled the mountain once more.

It was late and they decided to rest. They had a restless sleep and they had breakfast in the morning. Leo had some bread. The old lady kept drinking from her hip flask. They then continued going up the mountain. Around noon, they were high enough on the mountain that they could see the entire world before them.

Leo saw his village. Small, unremarkable, almost laughable from up here. Just a few houses, one as boring as the other, and small wisps of smoke rising above them. Nothing remarkable or memorable. But this got Leo thinking.

"Are there other villages in the world?", Leo asked.

"No". "Were there?"

"Yes". "When?"

"A long time ago. There used to be very big villages, called cities, once. Lots of people back then."

"What happened?"

"Incompetence or selfishness. One of the two," The old lady said.

She drank from her hip flask, her face grimaced a bit as she spoke.

"Say, lad, after you kill that beast and he's gone forever, do you think you'll be happy forever?"

"Yes," Leo said without skipping a beat.

"Is that so…" The old lady said.

They continued their search for the beast. They looked everywhere. They looked in caves and every crevice they could find, but the Chimera was not there. That thing must've gone further up, and so they scaled the mountain once more.

Today's search was also not fruitful. The beast was nowhere to be found, and so they rested for the day. This time, they woke to gray and sickly dawn. Leo was feeling a bit nauseous because the air smelt like metal and the daylight had a reddish hue to it. It looked and felt wrong.

"What is going on?" Leo asked.

The old lady shrugged and drank from her hip flask once more. Leo saw something in the ground. It was a silver-colored ground but looked alien to Leo.

"What is this?" Leo asked.

"How should I describe it… It is something from long ago," The old lady said.

"What does that even mean?"

The old lady shrugged and told Leo that he would not understand anyway. It was not long before Leo saw machines made from silver, glass. He saw tall towers of glass, with breathtaking shapes. It was alien to Leo, who used to see little wooden houses with straws for roofs.

"Who built these things?", Leo asked.

"Well, the New Gods, of course."

"These are astounding work. Why would they leave these behind?"

"All good things must come to an end. Sometimes, toys are no longer fun to play with."

As they scaled the mountains, Leo witness many more phenomena. All about them appeared weird glyphs and symbols in the air. Lights flashed in the distanced. The metallic reek grew thicker and stronger as they climbed. The sight was so alien to Leo that he thought he was on a different planet.

Eventually, they happened upon a clearing where a pedestal sat. Upon that pedestal was a pair of glasses. The old lady went to pick it up and handed it to Leo.

"Wear this," the old lady said, "These are the glasses you will understand the beast with."

"Glasses?" Leo said, "But my eyes are fine."

"You'd think that, and you'd be wrong." The old lady said and put them on Leo's face. Immediately, Leo was teleported from his body. His senses ascended above that of the gods and he saw the reality for what it really was. It was a tangle of fields and dimensions. He saw the height of time and the width of space. He saw that everything he ever knew was a point, a wave, and a joke. He understood everything and he understood how crazy everything really was.

He saw the shape of becoming and the dance of decline. He soon saw himself for what he really was. He was nothing but a spec on a bloc of this world, which was little more than a blemish on a fleck on the galaxy scale. Even that galaxy was nothing more than a grain of sand in a vast beach, which made up more grains of sand, and more grains of sand, and more grains of sand.

Eventually, the old lady removed his glasses. Leo gasped and fell on his bottom. It felt like having his soul ripped from his body and violently shoved back into his body.

"What the hell was that?" Leo asked, still breathless.

"It was the gift of the New Gods, way back when." She then gave Leo the glasses, "Keep these safe, hm?"

It was then Leo started to question who this old lady really was.

"Who are you?", Leo asked.

"Oh", she replied. "Who's anyone?"

And so their search for the Chimera continued. They looked everywhere. They looked in caves and every crevice they could find, but the Chimera was not there. That thing must've gone further up, and so they scaled the mountain once more.

Their search was once again not fruitful and so they rested at sundown. The next morning, they woke to see a beautiful view of Leo's village which was barely visible from up here.

Leo stood there for a moment and sighed.

"Where is everyone? It feels like the world is dead."

"The world IS dead, child." The old lady said.

"Why is the world dead?"

"Everyone was too clever for their own goods. Now, everyone is gone, except for your village."

"Where are they then"

"There." The old lady said and pointed up to the sky, "But that's enough history lesson. Come on, time's getting on."

And so they continued up the mountain. With the peak still impossibly high, and the village was starting to become less and less visible. But Leo's resolve had not wavered. That beast will die.

As they walked. Leo thought of his father once more. Once that beast was dead, Leo will return to the village. But what then? He thought that the days ahead of him would be empty and overcast, a very boring life. He wondered how his father had lived his life, what he had gone through. Perhaps his father had suffered the same thing when his father had passed away.

How did his father cope then? With no one to talk to, really. With no one to go fishing with. With no more silly dad jokes. It would be a very boring life. And Leo came to this world that made it better for him, but now he's gone and it was the beast's fault.

When Leo would find the beast, he would make sure that the beast suffered the same way the entire village did, tenfold.

Eventually, the duo happened upon a stream. The water was dark crimson and it reeked. It was then he realized that it was blood. That stream of blood became thicker and thicker as they trudged on. It was a river of blood. On the red-stained and scorched ground were coins and jewels, scepters, and rich and fancy clothes.

The air now no longer smelled of metal. Rather, it stank of death and glory. Eventually, they came upon yet another flat ground. In the middle of it was a large rock. Sat upon that rock was a sword, buried in the rock up to the hilt.

It was sticking out from the rock, hilt glowing bright crimson and purple and gold. The blade a beautiful silver. The duo approached the sword.

"Take it from the ground then, lad," The old lady said.

Leo approached the sword and observed its details.

"What is this?" Leo asked.

"This is the sword that you will kill the beast with."

Leo took a deep breath and gripped the sword. With a great effort, Leo wrenched the sword from the ground and brandished it.

Just as he did, pillars of flames and lightning leaped from the tip of his sword and setting the ground alight with a thunderous roar. Leo brandished it again and a swarm of locusts and wasps leaped from the tip, consuming everything in its path, leaving only clouds of dust in their wake. He bellowed a burst of great wicked laughter. It rang over the mountain, greater than the roar of the beast that Leo would slay.

Leo had never felt unimaginable power before. He now understood what it was like to be the gods. He knew what it was like to be weak and frail, subject to the wills and tyranny of the strong, to the evil of the beast.

But no longer did he had to stand for it. Everyone and everything will obey him now. The village elders, the oracles, the bullies, and the brutes. Even the beast will bow to him when the time came.

Leo laughed once more as he stood upon the mountain that was riddled with fire, lightning, and death. It was a symbol of his insurmountable rage for that beast who had robbed him of his beloved father.

"I shall always kill," he thought to himself. It was then he knew that no one could do anything to stop him. No one. Even the New Gods would be powerless against him. Even the New Gods would beg for mercy if they evoked his wrath. The Chimera would be too. And more than that, with a dastardly certainty he supposed that with this thing, he could end the world if he wanted.

The next day, Leo ate his bread and the old lady drank from her flask in silence. They started walking as usual. As they walked, Leo wondered and asked, "How long until we find the beast?"

The old woman drank, said nothing. Leo realized that the old lady had been drinking from the flask for the last few days and at no point did he see her get her refill.

"Isn't that thing empty already?", Leo said.

The old lady chuckled and turned the flask upside down. And out poured booze endlessly. Leo blinked, speechless.

"What is that? Are you one of the New Gods?", Leo said.

"It is one of the New Gods' makings", the old woman said.

"Well, what happened to the New Gods?"

"The beast", she said.

"It killed them?"

"Sure."

Leo blinked, confused. "It killed them? Then what chances do I have against it?"

"The thought hadn't crossed my mind", the old woman mumbled and shrugged casually, "You are still not prepared. We still need to collect a few more things here."

"Like what?", Leo said.

But already, he heard music; upbeat, calling to him.

They came on the remains of a great party; empty bottles, discarded trinkets.

"What happened here?", Leo said.

"Abandon", the old woman said.

In ruins of an old and ostentatious house, burnt partly to the ground, was a tankard that glowed. And inside the tankard was what looked, and smelled like mead.

"Go on", the old woman said. "Drink a little."

"What is it?", Leo said.

"This is the indulgence you will need to kill the beast and celebrate its death with."

And with that, Leo drank. And when the cup came away, the old woman grabbed Leo's hand and led him into a dance. Everything started to spin around them. Everything became blurry and Leo was lost to his senses, not really knowing what was going on as they danced.

"What's happening?!", Leo yelled.

And the old lady yelled, "That's it! Dance!"

And Leo and the old lady danced across the mountain, over the debauchery, and under the moon. And suddenly, Leo was not thinking of his father; or the beast, or the village.

"What if there's no point to anything?" the old woman sang. "Who cares?"

"Who cares?" Leo agreed.

"Tragedies happen, people die. It's all a game, it's all a facade!

"There's no salvation, no meaning!"

It was then Leo realized how things really were. That everything was suffering, and even that didn't matter. Everything was nothing but a joke. A joke that the New Gods were playing. Everything had no meaning except to amuse those higher beings with a sick taste for amusement.

Leo and the old lady danced across the mountains now, feet stepping in perfect sync, the stars spinning all around them. Leo's mind was lost to the world, but that didn't matter. Nothing really mattered. The song continued to echo across the mountains, well into the night, up until the sun rose above the horizon once more.

Leo woke with a throbbing head, and a mouth that tasted like nothing he had ever tasted before. The old woman was already up, smoking a pipe.

"All well?", she said. "Mm...", Leo mumbled.

"Was the dancing really necessary?", he said

The woman nodded. "Certainly was!"

"Come on, we're very close now. The beast can't hide forever."

It was then Leo had had it. He stood up and his face scowled.

"I'm staying until you tell me everything. What is going on here? You said you know everything, so answer me!"

But the old lady paid him no mind. She shrugged and got up, collected her things, and started to walk again.

"Whatever. Come on."

She started walking again. But Leo would not move. The old lady turned to him, rolled her eyes, and sighed.

"Fine, fine," she muttered. "What's the year?"

"Hmm... 507," Leo said.

"By your calendar, yes. By mine, it's the 30th century. You see, your ancestors, the New Gods, created magic, or at least that would be something you would describe it as. It is a powerful science that took a very long time to understand and master. And they became very powerful. Everything that we have here is artifacts from the New Gods. They are relics."

"Relics of what?"

"I'll show you."

"No!" Leo yelled, "No more games!"

The old woman gritted her teeth, took another deep breath, and said "Look! You're only doing all of this because you think you killed your father!"

Leo was quiet.

"Your father, he went over the barrier. Do you know why? Because he wanted to get you something special for your birthday. He remembered that you wanted a shooting star, and so he did go over the barrier. He found nothing, but he did find death. I know that you are having a hard time right now, but please don't take all this out on me."

Leo was taken aback. He was silent awhile, then said quietly, "How do you know that?"

The old lady rolled her eyes and shrugged.

"Like I said from the start. I know things. And I'm trying to help you here, so would you give a poor old woman a break?"

Seeing that there was no point in arguing about it anyway, Leo nodded and collected his stuff. The two continued to walk on in silence. Below, the village was almost invisible and the top of the mountain drew ever closer.

They turned a corner and came upon a picture of a king. Then a queen, then more. All portraits, showing proud faces that power and cruelty. Spoke of war and conquest. Spoke of brilliance and treachery. There were more pictures as they pushed forward.

Now, the pictures are that of tall glass building piercing the skies, large cities with so many people that Leo could have never imagined, all using weird devices and wearing funny clothes. All of that, countless years of history that Leo had never known, all was lost to time.

All of that was long forgotten, like a dream. These pictures served as a testament to the time when countless others like Leo had existed in harmony, on this little planet called Earth, nothing larger than a speck of dust in the infinite vastness of space. Even so, they held out. They held out against the hostile cosmos and yet worse threats that lurked, within themselves. And somehow, for a long time, against all odds and sense, they did hold out. Slowly but surely, they got better and better, just like a toddler who attempts to walk.

Then, for some reason, devolving, again. The great sleep; the great forgetting. Sent to bed, with no supper. Then decline, then savagery, then dust. No one knew what. No one knew why. No one knew how it all happened. It was the great rise, and an equally tragic fall from grace to grim.

And ahead, Leo spied was a pair of armored boots. It was a beautiful pair of silver boots with intricate carvings yet had a sturdy and comfortable feel to it.

"There," the old lady said. "The boots will protect you from the beast. With it, you are invulnerable, even to death itself. No disease can harm you. No blade can pierce your skin. Nothing can even pull a single strand of hair off your head. The beast cannot harm you now."

They fitted perfectly.

"And one more thing," the old woman said. She took from her shawl a necklace. And on the necklace was a locket, and in the locket was a picture of Leo's father. She put the necklace over his head.

"To remember," she said.

After all of that, Leo felt that he was ready for the battle ahead. It was a long and arduous journey, but he knew it would only be a short walk, now. The peak was just a few yards away. It was only a small plateau, and the wind was high here. And it was raining. And there, sat the beast. Its back turned to Leo, staring off into the dead wilderness below.

"There you are," the old woman said. "Do as you will."

With the glasses of the New Gods on his face, he saw the beast in its essence. Its black heart, its cunning mind, its contempt for the last remaining humans. Leo approached, silently. His heart and his temples, his eyes wide, his hand clutching the locket of his father. And he thought of his father then. He thought of the man dead; thought of the futility of death.

And he closed his eyes and screamed, and brought the sword down with such power that it struck a grating chord out into the rain. And rang all the way back to the mountain's base. He opened his eyes. The beast was gone. Leo turned around to the old woman, confused.

"Where did he go? Did you see him?" He asked.

"No," said the old lady who shrugged as if it was the most normal thing in the world. Leo was even more confused until the woman said, "I didn't see him, because he doesn't exist."

The rain was getting heavier. Leo stood there, dumbfounded. His armor creaked weakly as the rain tapped on its surface. Finally, the old lady said.

"Did you really think that there is such a beast? Do you think that there exists a beast that is the center of all your misery? Do you honestly think that the world is so simple that every of your ailment is caused by a single monster?"

"God, what is wrong with all of you? You have everything, you know that? And you spit on it. You had everything, you like living in some enormous mansion, and one day you see a chipped brick so you want to tear everything down and build another mansion. You got everything down there, you know? I gave you everything you'll ever need."

"You got food, life, peace, and yet all of you are unhappy. Do you have any idea how hard it is to be a god?"

Leo stood there in silence and he understood what she meant. As they stood, on the skyline appeared shimmering, and translucent buildings. High-technology and science.

The old lady sighed and continued, "They had everything they could have ever imagined, you know?"

"Your ancestors, that is. Still, they were miserable because of that one thing they could not have. They could not have the protection from the beast. It haunted them for eons. That beast, though you see it was a Chimera, is actually the messenger of misery, chaos, and death."

"And your ancestors tried everything they could to slay that beast. They tried sending it away with perfect knowledge, they tried killing it with ultimate power, they tried forgetting it with abandon, they tried living longer, they tried clinging to each other; The spectacles, sword, tankard, armor, and necklace."

"And they looked everywhere. They looked in caves and every crevice they could find, but the Chimera was not there. That thing must've gone further up, and so they climbed further and further and further and yet found nothing. The Chimera was not there because it does not exist. It was just them in the universe, and they were still miserable."

"So the New Gods are all gone now. All except me. And your species is gone too, now. Everyone except your village, the old yet simple way of life. It was a beautiful one, too. You are all here because I keep you around. I chose to do that because it reminds me of how my people were once."

"I'm sorry your father is gone. I'm sorry you'll never see him again. But you are not alone here. You got me, and everyone in the village. They all love you. And here you are, screaming at the wind on a mountain. Bad things happen, Leo. They always do and the reasons for them are complicated."

"There is no exact one thing that is responsible for all your misery. If there is, you would not be here. No one thing causes all your sadness and misery. And there'll never come a time when everything lasts forever, nothing hurts ever again. It's not gone yet. It won't be, for ages. Don't waste your time on something you cannot control. Make your peace and do your best. Say goodbye."

She took the jam jar out of Leo's satchel and gave it to him. She put her arm around his shoulder. Slowly, Leo opened the jar. And the wind took the ashes of his father and flung them out over the mountain.

They stood in silence for a while to honor Leo's father's passing.

"When you look at it, it is funny." The old lady said to break the silence, "We might be the only living being who cannot be perpetually happy. Give a cat a fish and fluff and it's content for the rest of its life. We, on the other hand, though we ruled the galaxy, a long time ago, we still quarreled over who got more ice cream for dessert."

"So, go home, Leo. You don't need to be an honorable hero, a mighty warrior, or a great sage. Just live a while and be good to others. That is heroic enough. That is how things should be done. In fact, if you want to keep the glasses, sword, tankard, and armor, you can take over the world if you want."

"No," Leo said, "I don't need these. They won't make me happy."

"Good choice," The old lady said.

Leo asked the old lady whether he was the first ever to have come up here, to slay the beast, to see the old lady. But she shook her head sighed in frustration.

"Everyone from the village came up. One by one. I gave them all the same treatment; they all went back down. Even your father. In fact, he asked a lot of silly questions. Maybe you got that part of him."

"But I hope that you are the last person to ever come up here. So, Leo, go home and just be a normal human. The universe, as you already saw, is vast and does not care about you. But everyone down here does. We care about you. Your village, your family, me, we really do."

"Remember your dad. Love him always. God knows he loved you. If you'd like, you can visit me in the forest. We can hang out and maybe drink together and remember your father, together."

Leo smiled and took off the glasses, and the armor, and the tankard, and laid the sword down on the ground. All except the necklace.

"Can I keep the necklace?", he said.

The old lady nodded, "That and the memories. They are yours and no one can take that away from you. Not me. Not the beast. Not the universe. Not the New Gods."

The ashes were gone now, all sank into the ground. Leo took a deep breath and let that reality sink in, the fact that his father had passed, that it was outside his control. He understood the inevitability of misery, yet he knew that it only made happiness worthwhile, for what is happiness without misery? What is light without darkness? What is good without bad? One gave the other purpose. One gave the other meaning.

The sky was clear and fine. Leo set off, back down the last mountain, bound for his village. While it was not a difficult journey, it would be a long one. But Leo did not mind so much now. It would give him some more time to remember his father, and what he had learned from this journey.

He eventually arrived at the village and everyone gathered, voicing their worries for Leo who had been gone for god knows how long. But Leo told them that he had been up the mountain. Everyone understood what he meant immediately. They all said that they had gone up the mountain, met the same old lady, and attempted to slay the same old beast.

The beast had always been there. Everyone hated it, but there was nothing they could do about it. No one could ever defeat the beast, but that was quite alright. The villagers had everyone and to all of them, that would be enough. It would not be nearly enough for eternal happiness, but what they had was enough for a peaceful life.

And so Leo, having learned a very valuable lesson that day, went back to his home and fell asleep the moment his head hit the pillow. It was a long and arduous day. But the next time he woke, he would make sure to thank the villagers for everything they had done for him. He would make sure to be a decent human and he believed that it would be enough to make his father happy.

END OF MEDITATIONS

Hello! We really hope you enjoyed listening to these meditations, we poured our heart and soul into making these guided meditations as amazing as possible, as well as making them as helpful as possible for you, the listener. Each Meditation and was crafted with complete care and attention to help you enter a deep state of relaxation, and achieve the intended goal of the meditation, whether it was to help you reduce anxiety, relieve depression symptoms, or help you get that essential healing sleep your body is in need of. If you have enjoyed this book, we would really appreciate if you could leave us a review on Audible. Reviews really help us more than anything else. They help our books be seen by more and more people, and as a result help more and more people with these Guided Meditations, which is the mission we are on, to help as many people as possible unlock their natural happiness that is inherent to them by utilizing the power of Meditation, and we believe our Guided meditations are the perfect tool to help people do that.

So, if you have enjoyed these Guided Meditations, it would mean the absolute world to us if you could simply leave us a written review telling us what parts you enjoyed most, what meditations helped you the most, and exactly what you want to see more of from us in the future.

Once again, thank you for listening, and remember these meditations can be enjoyed and repeated time and time again, and we will always have more and more meditations, bedtime stories and Hypnosis in the works, so keep an eye out for that.

We hope you have an amazing day!

www.ingramcontent.com/pod-product-compliance
Lightning Source LLC
Chambersburg PA
CBHW081411080526